To my mum, Isabel

The Spanish Pantry

José Pizarro

Quadrille

Contents

Introduction

When I think of the 'Spanish pantry', I'm stirred by numerous vivid childhood memories that have shaped my understanding of Spanish cuisine. Straight away I remember the comforting aroma of tomatoes gently simmering on my mother's stove, filling our home with the scent of summer. She would carefully peel, chop and cook them down, preserving them to last us through the winter months. These aromas permeated our home and every meal was suffused with Spanish flavours. Each dish held echoes of the past – our history on a plate, embodying the passion, labour and love for the ingredients, as well as a respect for the journey of bringing those ingredients from seed to plate.

Tomatoes are the taste of Spanish sunshine but peppers too have a cherished place in my memories. I remember how we would harvest them from my dad's vegetable garden and take them to the village bakery where, in wood-fired ovens, they were transformed into sweet, smoky perfection, their skins turning a glorious golden brown as they caramelised. I can still see the sacks of roasted peppers, lined up and waiting to be peeled, so that their flesh could be preserved according to our traditions.

In our cellar, large white onions would hang in long strings, their papery skins rustling in the quiet, while the broad beans were carefully stored to maintain their super-fresh flavour. I can also lovingly recall the most significant event of the year in our small rural village: the annual *matanza*. This traditional pig slaughter was a community effort, drawing the extended family and friends together to prepare jamón, chorizo and other delicacies for preservation. These rural rituals did more than secure our winter food supplies; they preserved a way of life, embedding every ingredient with meaning and purpose. Our deep appreciation for the care and effort that went into filling our pantry was as rich as the flavours themselves.

The Spanish pantry is a vibrant tapestry of flavours, colours and textures, deeply rooted in local traditions and enriched by a history of global influence. Many ingredients that seem quintessentially Spanish, like tomatoes and peppers, have journeys that began far from our shores, arriving from the Americas in the 16th century as exotic gifts for the monarchy. Peppers, in particular, were embraced by the ingenuity of monks in the monasteries

of Guadalupe and Yuste in Extremadura, who dried and smoked them, grinding them into what we now cherish as the very best pimentón de la Vera. This smoky pimentón became a defining element in chorizo, stews and marinades, and the appreciation echoes far beyond the shores of Spain.

My fondest memories have led me to choose twelve ultimate ingredients that I think frame the heart and soul of Spanish cuisine. Twelve ingredients telling a unique story, woven into the fabric of Spanish cooking. These essentials are more than just staples; they are the culinary foundations upon which countless traditional recipes stand, and an invitation to experiment with creativity in the kitchen.

Bursting with a rich, earthy sweetness, **tomatoes** are indispensable, transforming dishes to a unique style. From the velvety smoothness of gazpacho to the slow-cooked perfection of sofrito, this is such a versatile ingredient that

it brings a ray of sunshine into the kitchen all year round. The diversity of **peppers**, from the subtle sweetness of roasted piquillos to the bold heat of dried ñoras, add layers of flavour and depth to our dishes.

The much-revered **jamón**, with its deep nuttiness and tender, melt-in-the-mouth texture, creates moments of indulgence, representing the pinnacle of Spanish craftsmanship. Jamón is so divine that it can elevate even a simple piece of bread into a mouthful of heaven. Likewise, **chorizo**, robust with smoky paprika and garlic, tells the story of rural ingenuity where preservation techniques turn simple ingredients into bold, remarkable flavours.

Saffron, our 'golden treasure,' is the fine elegant thread that infuses many of our most-loved dishes. Its delicate aroma and vibrant colour can transform a simple paella into a thing of beauty, such is the power of a tiny pinch. **Onions**, sometimes overlooked but completely indispensable, are the understated hero of Spanish cooking. The range of sweet and savoury onions form the base of many recipes, from rich stews to *tortilla de patatas* (page 19). **Chickpeas**, my personal favourite, offer their golden, nutty richness to the comforting *Cocido madrileño* as well as refreshing salads. **Beans**, a staple in traditional dishes like the hearty *fabada Asturiana* (page 191), provide both substance and a subtle flavour that perfectly complements the bold spices of our cuisine. **Rice**, cultivated in the sun-drenched fields of Valencia, is foundational, its grains capturing the essence of Spain's most iconic recipes.

Firm yet creamy, **Manchego** cheese is Spain on a plate. Made from sheep's milk in the heart of La Mancha, this cheese represents the simple, timeless pleasure of Spanish dining. Paired with a drizzle of honey or a slice of quince, it's pure perfection. **Almonds** bring their subtle sweetness and unique texture to Spanish cuisine. Ground into sauces like romesco, stirred into desserts like *tarta de Santiago*, or scattered over salads, they add texture and balance.

Citrus fruits bring liveliness and vibrancy. Their tangy zest lifts sauces and dressings to another level, while the juicy sweetness of plump fruit finds its way into desserts and marinades. A squeeze of lemon over seafood or a dash of orange in a salad creates vibrancy and harmony.

These ingredients, each with its own story and place in our heritage, constitute the backbone of the Spanish pantry and are testament to the land and the people who have nurtured them through the generations. They are the foundations of countless traditional recipes and an invitation to creativity and exploration in the kitchen, leading us through the rich, diverse and delicious landscape of Spanish cooking.

Onions

Onions are undoubtedly the major staple in Spanish cooking, showing up in almost every traditional recipe and much loved for the flavour and richness they bring to dishes. They're valued not only for their taste but also because they store well, making them available throughout the year. Originally thought to have come from Central Asia, onions were introduced to Spain by the Romans, who spread their cultivation across their empire, including the Iberian Peninsula. Later, under Islamic rule, the Moors improved onion farming with new irrigation methods, helping the onions grow even better in the Spanish climate.

Onions quickly became a pantry essential in Spain, especially valuable in the days before fridges. In winter, when fresh vegetables were scarce, onions were key for adding flavour to soups, stews and other warming dishes, with a balanced profile of mild heat with an earthy savoury-sweetness, providing depth.

I think one of the best ways that onions are used in Spain is in sofrito, a base made by slowly caramelising the onions with garlic, tomatoes and olive oil. This mix helps the onions lose their rawness, depending on the variety, and is the foundation of many Spanish dishes, like Griddled spring onion tortilla (page 19) – *tortilla de patatas* – which I always prefer made with onions. In this book I have created a new recipe using spring onions, which is a real winner! Slow-cooking the onions brings out their natural sweetness, nuttiness and a delicate umami flavour. Cooking spring onions mellows out any sharpness but retains the bright, fresh crispiness – perfect for tortillas, lazy omelettes and soups.

Today, I would say that onions are arguably the single most important pantry item in Spain, anchoring flavours in every dish. Whether raw, sautéed, caramelised, grilled or roasted, they are the base of many favourite dishes that makes Spanish cuisine so full of flavour.

The Spanish Pantry

Tuna with sticky caramelised onions

- Serves 4
- Takes 1 hour 20 minutes

We're very fortunate to have our home, Iris, within touching distance of the *almadrabas* in the Cádiz region. The ancient technique of *almadraba* fishing has been practised for over three thousand years along the Cádiz coast. Introduced by the Phoenicians, this method continued throughout the Roman and Moorish eras. Unfortunately, by the 1970s, bluefin tuna was little appreciated, leading to a significant decline in the traditional method and consequently devastating towns that relied on it. Today, four locations in Cádiz – Barbate, Zahara, Tarifa and Conil – have revived the traditional *almadraba* technique.

Originally, the *almadraba* involved nets anchored on either side of the Strait of Gibraltar, capturing tuna as they migrated from the cold Atlantic into the Mediterranean during springtime to spawn in warmer waters. This annual migration creates significant concentrations of bluefin tuna near the entrance to the Mediterranean, between Spain and Morocco. Unfortunately, due to the predictability of their migration and a renewed demand for the fish in restaurants from Madrid to Tokyo and New York, bluefin tuna was overfished to the point of endangerment. Strictly enforced quotas and restrictions aimed at protecting the population have resulted in numbers beginning to recover since 2010. The lesson for us in this is that if we look after the planet, the planet can recover from all the mistakes we have made.

This recipe is one of my favourites that we love to cook and enjoy at Iris. Originally a fisherman's dish, this version comes from my dear friend Pepi, who is married to Pablo Crespo from a Gadira family who own several *almadrabas*. He knows more about tuna, and fishing, than anyone else I know.

My twist on this regional favourite is to spice the stock with local fennel seed, chilli and oregano. This tuna is rich in aromas and flavours that perfectly complement the spices, and I get very excited about how much it truly elevates the taste of the tuna!

Recipe continues overleaf

100ml (3½fl oz/scant ½ cup) olive oil
4 large Spanish onions, finely sliced
3 garlic cloves, bashed
2 bay leaves
4 sprigs of oregano
pinch of chilli flakes
1 tsp fennel seeds
½ tsp sweet smoked pimentón
100ml (3½fl oz/scant ½ cup) fino
    sherry or white wine
1 tbsp sherry vinegar
250ml (8½fl oz/1 cup) fresh fish stock
300g (10½oz) fresh tuna, cut into
    1.5cm (⅝in) cubes
crusty bread, to serve

Heat the oil in a pan over a low heat, add the onions, then cover with a piece of baking parchment and a lid and cook very gently for 30 minutes.

Remove the lid and paper, then add the garlic, bay leaves oregano, chilli and fennel seeds and continue to cook down for about 25 minutes until golden and sticky.

Add the pimentón and sherry and simmer, stirring, to reduce completely to a thick sauce. Add the sherry vinegar, then one-third of the fish stock and allow to completely reduce. Repeat this process twice more, stopping when the last stock addition has reduced by about half.

Add the pieces of tuna to the pan, cover and cook for 3–4 minutes until just cooked through and the onions are juicy but not runny. Serve with crusty bread.

Tip

If you can make your own fish stock, it makes all the difference. Cover the bones of a couple of fish (you can save them from other recipes you make and keep in the freezer until you have enough to make stock) and the shells from about 500g (1lb 2oz) of prawns (shrimp) with water and add a bay leaf, a couple of sprigs of oregano and a teaspoon of fennel seeds. Bring to the boil, then simmer for 30 minutes before draining and using or cooling and freezing.

Pickled baby onions with chicken liver pâté

- Serves 6–8 (makes 2 × 375g/1lb jars)
- Takes 1½ hours plus overnight and marinating

Baby onions weren't common when I was a child, and I hadn't used them until I started working with my friends Emma and Julio at Chapin de la Reina, outside Madrid. We cooked them in various dishes, though we never pickled them and, in fact, I didn't pickle much at all until moving to the UK. These pickled onions need at least a month to reach their perfect flavour, but every single day of waiting is worth it.

A fino en rama will be the perfect match for this; it will balance the earthy flavours from the liver with the acidity of the pickled onions.

400g (14oz) small baby onions or pearl onions
20g (¾oz) sea salt
500ml (17fl oz/2 cups) distilled white vinegar
250ml (8½fl oz/1 cup) sherry vinegar
200g (7oz/heaped 1 cup) caster (superfine) sugar
2 tbsp coriander seeds
1 tbsp black peppercorns

For the liver pâté
300g (10½oz) free-range chicken livers
3 tbsp brandy
pared zest of 1 orange
1 chilli, halved
2 tbsp olive oil
200g (7oz) unsalted butter, melted, plus 50g (2oz) for clarifying
flaky sea salt and freshly ground black pepper

Tips

Once opened, the onions will keep in the fridge for several months.

The pâté would also be delicious served with Sweet citrus jelly (page 133).

To pickle the onions, place the onions in a bowl and pour over a kettle full of boiling water. Leave to stand until cool, then drain, peel and top and bottom the onions. Sprinkle them with the salt and leave overnight.

The next day, rinse them and pat dry then put into sterilised jars (page 32).

Heat the vinegars with the sugar until hot but not boiling, then pour over the onions. Toast the coriander seeds and peppercorns in a dry frying pan (skillet) until fragrant, then add them to the jars. Seal and leave for at least 1 month.

To make the liver pâté, put the livers in a dish with the brandy, orange zest and chilli and marinate in the fridge for 1 hour. Remove the livers and pat them dry, reserving the brandy.

Heat the oil in a large pan, season the livers with salt and pepper, add them to the pan and fry over a high heat for about 2 minutes on each side until browned. Add the reserved brandy and allow it to cook until it has almost all evaporated.

Discard the orange and chilli, then tip the livers into a food processor and blitz until smooth. With the motor running, gradually whiz in the melted butter until it has all been incorporated. Push the mixture through a sieve into a bowl, then divide among 6 ramekins.

Melt the remaining butter and discard the milk solids. Pour the clarified butter over the little ramekins and chill for at least 5 hours before serving with toasts and the pickled onions.

Griddled spring onion tortilla

- Serves 4
- Takes 30 minutes

Tortilla de patatas is a classic blend of eggs and potatoes but here's the eternal debate: onions or no onions. Drum roll … in my family it's … always onions!

The reason is that this twist is just so good, especially when using griddled spring onions for a smoky, slightly charred flavour that I absolutely love. This recipe honours the basics but adds a creative twist. What we have here is tender potatoes and spring onions for a tortilla that's just set on the inside and golden on the outside. I think this version celebrates tradition while adding a subtle, modern edge. Yes, onions in my tortilla! In fairness, here they are caramelised spring onions. No more debate please, everyone's happy, just the way I like it.

10 spring onions (scallions), trimmed
120ml (4fl oz/½ cup) olive oil
175g (6oz) red-skinned potatoes, peeled and finely sliced
4 large free-range eggs
75ml (2½fl oz/scant ⅓ cup) extra virgin olive oil
flaky sea salt and freshly ground black pepper

Heat a griddle pan over a high heat. Toss the spring onions in 2 tablespoons of the olive oil and griddle until tender and charred. Remove from the pan, season with salt and pepper and chop the spring onions.

Heat the remaining olive oil in an 18–20cm (7–8in) non-stick frying pan (skillet) and cook the potatoes very gently for 10 minutes until just tender.

Beat the eggs with plenty of salt and pepper. Drain the potatoes, reserving the oil, and, while they are still warm, toss them and the spring onions with the eggs.

Put 2 tablespoons of oil back into the pan and place over a medium heat. Pour in the egg and potato mixture then jiggle the pan until the eggs start to set around the edges. Reduce the heat to low and cook for 5–6 minutes until the eggs are almost but not quite set.

Invert the pan onto a flat board, then quickly slide the tortilla back into the pan – it might ooze a little but don't worry as it will re-form once you return it to the pan. Place back on the heat and with a spatula, tuck the edges of the tortilla under themselves to create the classic rounded edge. Continue to cook for another 3–4 minutes.

Turn the tortilla out onto a plate and serve.

Spanish onion soup

- Serves 6
- Takes 1¼ hours

This is just so good! In many of my recipes for soups, I typically advise cooking onions slowly under a lid to achieve a soft texture. However, for this recipe, I allow the onions to caramelise with pimentón until they become sticky and rich. Understanding how varying the cooking time and heat affects onions is crucial. Cooking them slowly allows their natural sugars to gently emerge, resulting in a soft, mellow flavour. On the other hand, a higher heat brings out a deeper, more intense sweetness as the sugars caramelise, adding a rich complexity to the dish. The smoky flavour from the pimentón de la Vera is just sublime and perfect with a poached egg on top and a glass of oloroso sherry – very important!

100ml (3½fl oz/scant ½ cup) olive oil
5 large onions, finely sliced
4 garlic cloves, sliced
2 tbsp light soft brown sugar
1 bay leaf
4 sprigs of oregano
1 tsp sweet smoked pimentón de la Vera
125ml (4fl oz/½ cup) oloroso sherry
1 litre (34fl oz/4 cups) fresh chicken stock
1 tbsp cider vinegar
6 free-range eggs
6 small slices of bread, torn into pieces
120g (4oz) Manchego, grated
flaky sea salt and freshly ground black pepper

Heat 3 tablespoons of the oil in a large flameproof casserole or pan and add the onions and garlic. Cover and cook very gently for 1 hour until they are super-soft and tender, stirring occasionally.

Season with salt and pepper and add the sugar, bay leaf, oregano and pimentón and cook, uncovered, for a further 45–60 minutes until deeply golden and sticky, stirring regularly so it doesn't stick to the pan.

Add the sherry and bubble for about 5 minutes, then add the chicken stock and simmer for 15 minutes. Add the vinegar and simmer for 5 minutes more.

Meanwhile, poach the eggs in a pan of barely simmering water.

Heat the remaining oil in a frying pan (skillet) and fry the bread until golden and crisp on one side. Flip the bread, season with salt and top with Manchego. Cover with a lid and allow the cheese to melt a little, then remove from the heat.

Spoon the soup into bowls, top with the cheese bread and a poached egg and serve.

The Spanish Pantry

Chicken and onions

- Serves 4
- Takes 2½ hours

Whenever I cook this recipe, I have the fondest memories of being at home with my mum, Isabel, and, thinking about it, most of my memories of this dish are of being in my mum's house, probably because it's one of the family's favourite dishes. The simplest things in life are often the best. The reason this is such a big hit at home, and everyone raves about it when Mum makes it, is because it's all about her signature slow cooking, and this one is the ultimate test! The chicken turns out tasting as if it's been roasted: juicy, tender and succulent. Any leftovers – although there aren't many when Isabel makes it – are absolutely perfect for making great croqueta.

Enjoy it with a glass of white Rioja.

4 tbsp olive oil
3 large onions, finely sliced
6 garlic cloves, left whole
4 free-range chicken legs
2 bay leaves
180ml (6fl oz/¾ cup) dry white wine
handful of flat-leaf parsley, leaves picked, to garnish
flaky sea salt and freshly ground black pepper
crusty bread and extra virgin olive oil, to serve

Heat the olive oil in a pan, add the onions and garlic and cook for a couple of minutes to just coat all over in the oil. Season the chicken really well with salt and pepper, then add it to the pan with the bay leaves and toss to coat in the oil. Cover and cook over a low heat for 30 minutes.

Add the wine and re-cover. Continue to cook for a further 2 hours until the chicken is really tender and juicy. Scatter with parsley and serve with crusty bread and a good drizzle of extra virgin olive oil.

The Spanish Pantry

Seared steak with roasted red onions and spring onion salsa

- Serves 4
- Takes 45 minutes

When I take my friends or guests to Barbate market to do some shopping, they never believe me when we drive along the coastal road and I tell them to look out for the cows bathing in the sea on Barbate beach! But they are there! This impressive breed is called Retinta, a local breed known for its excellent, high-quality meat, especially from matured cattle. All the cuts of this spectacular animal are wonderful, but the chops, that we call *chuletón,* are always a winner for me.

They pair beautifully with a glass of robust Priorat; its full body and particular notes complement, and stand up to, the rich flavours of the meat.

4 large red onions, cut into wedges
3 tbsp olive oil, plus extra for drizzling
5 sprigs of thyme
2 × 300g (10½oz) sirloin steaks
  (or 4 × 150g (5oz) steaks)

For the salsa
1 tbsp olive oil
1 bunch of spring onions (scallions)
250g (9oz) cherry tomatoes, finely
  chopped
½ large cucumber, deseeded and
  finely diced
good pinch of chilli flakes
2 tbsp sherry vinegar
4 tbsp extra virgin olive oil, for
  drizzling
flaky sea salt and freshly ground
  black pepper

Preheat the oven to 160°C fan (180°C/350°F/gas 4).

Put the onions on a large baking sheet, drizzle with 3 tablespoons of olive oil and toss with the thyme and plenty of salt and pepper. Roast for 30 minutes, turning once or twice, until tender and sticky.

Meanwhile, make the salsa. Heat the olive oil in a large pan and fry all but 3 of the spring onions until they are lightly charred. Allow to cool, then finely chop them and the raw spring onions and mix with the rest of the ingredients for the salsa in a bowl. Set aside to macerate.

Season the steak with salt and pepper and drizzle with olive oil. Heat a large griddle or heavy-based pan over a high heat. Sear the steak for 2–3 minutes on each side (depending on thickness) until charred but still pink. Allow to rest for 5 minutes.

Arrange the onions on a platter, slice the steak and lay it on top of the onions. Add any resting juices to the salsa, then spoon this over the steak and serve.

Salted anchovy and onion tart

- Serves 6
- Takes 1 hour

This tart encapsulates the most harmonious blend of garlic and onions that I can imagine, both of which are essentials in Spanish cuisine. Instead of using bell peppers for sweetness that I sometimes use, I've opted here for a dash of chilli flakes to inject a decent kick into the dish. The result is a bold and vibrant flavour that makes this tart a perfect snack for social gatherings, or an impressive starter. Paired beautifully with a simple red onion and herb salad, this recipe also highlights the robust character of anchovies, especially when their rich oil is included in the caramelisation of the onions. Enjoy a slice of Spain from your kitchen!

3 tbsp olive oil
3 medium onions, finely sliced
3 garlic cloves, finely sliced
5 sprigs of oregano, leaves stripped
pinch of chilli flakes
375g (13oz) sheet of puff pastry
2 × 29g (1oz) tins of anchovies in olive
 oil, drained
flaky sea salt and freshly ground
 black pepper
green salad, to serve

Heat the oil in a pan and gently fry the onions, garlic, oregano and chilli flakes for 25–30 minutes until soft and golden. Season well with salt and pepper. Allow to cool.

Preheat the oven to 180°C fan (200°C/400°F/gas 6).

Unroll the pastry, place on a baking sheet and score a line around the inside about 1.5cm (⅝in) from the edge. Spread the sticky onions all over the middle, then arrange the anchovies over the top.

Bake for 20–25 minutes until golden and crisp. Serve with a green salad.

Oysters with sherry vinegar
and red spring onion vinaigrette

- Serves 4
- Takes 10 minutes plus shucking the oysters

During the photoshoot at our home in Iris, some dear friends dropped by with an incredible gift of wild-harvested oysters from Conil de la Frontera, just a coastal stretch away. These exquisite oysters, plucked from the cold and powerful currents of the Atlantic ocean, offer a perfect balance of salty and sweet flavours – testament to the pristine conditions of their natural habitat. These oysters were a perfect addition to a memorable day, and even received my mum's coveted seal of approval! To complement their fresh brininess, I prepared a vinaigrette by blending finely chopped red spring onions with sherry vinegar and a squeeze of lemon. This dressing not only enhances the oysters' natural flavours but also introduces some necessary acidity that balances mineral sweetness beautifully. Enjoy this simple but sophisticated dish that brings a taste of the ocean right to your table.

2 dozen oysters
bunch of red spring onions (scallions), trimmed and very finely chopped
75ml (2½fl oz/scant ⅓ cup) sherry vinegar
juice of ½ lemon

Arrange the oysters on a plate.

Mix the spring onions with the sherry vinegar and lemon juice. Spoon the vinaigrette over the oysters and serve.

Tip

If you can't find red spring onions you can use a mix of banana shallots and green spring onions instead.

Tomatoes

Tomatoes are one of the most revered ingredients in Spain today, but getting to this point was far from straightforward. When they first arrived from the Americas in the early 16th century, likely brought by Spanish conquistadors, tomatoes were more of a curiosity than a kitchen staple. Their bright red colour and unusual shape made some people cautious about eating them, thinking they could be toxic. So, at first, they were grown mostly as decorative plants, adding a bit of exotic flair to Spanish gardens without anyone daring to eat them.

Eventually, people became curious enough to start experimenting, and it didn't take long to realise that tomatoes weren't just safe, they were delicious. From then on, they became a huge part of Spanish cooking. Now, they're at the heart of so many classic dishes. Some of the greatest include gazpacho, that cold, refreshing tomato soup that is so perfect for hot summer days, or Chilled roast tomato soup with figs (page 43), where the sweetness of the fruit and the tang of the tomatoes combine to create the most amazing flavours. In salads, soups, or cooked down into rich sauces, tomatoes bring a brightness and unique tang to Spanish cuisine that's hard to beat.

For my family, tomatoes have always been a staple, and they feature in a much-cherished personal tale. Around 25 years ago, my dad visited me in London and absolutely loved the little cherry tomatoes I was using. He had the idea to take those cherry tomatoes back from London to plant in our vegetable garden to see how they'd fare. They weren't at all common in our area at the time, but he loved their sweetness, and snackable size, and thought they'd be perfect for salads or just eating straight off the vine. He was delighted that the cherry tomatoes absolutely took off in his garden, with plentiful yields throughout the summer. They grew alongside the more traditional varieties, adding something special to our meals. In fact, my brother Antonio is still propagating cherry tomatoes to this very day from those my dad took back from London.

Home-preserved chopped tomatoes

- Makes 6 × 400g (14oz) jars
- Takes 1½ hours

Opening a jar of preserved tomatoes is like rewinding the recording of memory that ties me back to the day they were made. I recall the company, the weather, and what we were doing before and afterwards on that day. While I typically preserve my tomatoes plainly, to allow for culinary flexibility, adding herbs like rosemary or oregano during the preservation process can infuse them with additional flavours suited to your taste.

2.5kg (5lb 10oz) ripe plum tomatoes
3 tbsp cider vinegar
1 tbsp fine sea salt

Make a small cross in the bottom of each tomato with a sharp knife. Bring a large pot of water to the boil, then drop in the tomatoes a few at a time for about 30 seconds. Remove with a slotted spoon and plunge into a bowl of iced water.

Once cool, you can easily peel the skins off the tomatoes. Chop the flesh, retaining as much juice as you can.

Mix the tomato flesh with the vinegar and salt, then divide among your sterilised jars (see Tips below), leaving about 1–2cm (½–¾in) space at the top. Seal with the lids. Bring a large pan of water to the boil and place the jars into the water so they are submerged. You may need more than one pan or to do it in batches. Boil for about 45 minutes. Carefully remove from the water and leave to cool. You will hear them pop as the air seals in the jars and the lid indents pop in. Store in a cool dark place.

Tips

You can sterilise jars in the dishwasher or by washing in hot soapy water, then filling with boiling water from a kettle and drying on your lowest oven temperature.

You can try adding some chopped herbs – rosemary, basil or oregano, for example – to vary your options. The tomatoes can be stored for 6 months.

Luxurious tomato sauce

- Makes 800g (1lb 12oz)
- Takes 1 hour

Keeping this gorgeous tomato preserve in your pantry is a total game-changer. It's incredibly versatile – you can use it as a robust base for braised meats, a rich sauce for *albóndigas* (meatballs) or a lovely complement to pan-fried chicken or mackerel. It transforms a simple dish of fried eggs into something extraordinary and totally delicious!

100ml (3½fl oz/scant ½ cup) olive oil
1 white onion, very finely chopped
1 celery stalk, very finely chopped
1 carrot, very finely chopped
4 garlic cloves, peeled
2 bay leaves
150ml (5fl oz/scant ⅔ cup) fino sherry
   or dry white wine
2 × 400g (14oz) jars of Home-
   preserved chopped tomatoes
   (page 32) or tins of chopped
   tomatoes
2 tbsp tomato purée (paste)
flaky sea salt and freshly ground
   black pepper

Heat the oil in a large pan and gently fry the onion, celery and carrot for 10 minutes until soft.

Add the garlic and bay leaves and cook for a further 1 minute, then add the fino sherry and simmer to reduce by half, stirring occasionally.

Add the tomatoes and tomato purée and season well with salt and pepper. Simmer very gently for 30–40 minutes, stirring occasionally, until you have a thick, luscious tomato sauce.

Tip

The sauce will keep in the fridge for 2–3 days or you can freeze until needed for up to 3 months.

The Spanish Pantry

Triple tomato salad

- Serves 4–6
- Takes 30 minutes

This salad is a celebration of colours and flavours, perfect for lighting up any dinner party table or social event. Here, a medley of heirloom and sun-blushed tomatoes lays the foundation, creating a visually impressive display. Each slice offers a unique texture and a burst of flavour, from the juicy freshness of the heirloom varieties to the deeper, concentrated sweetness of the sun-blushed tomatoes. Adding fresh basil enhances the dish with fragrant notes, while a drizzle of extra virgin olive oil brings everything together in harmony.

800g (1lb 12oz) ripe heirloom
   tomatoes, sliced
10 sun-blushed tomatoes, sliced
very large handful of basil leaves
120g (4oz) shavings of payoyo or
   other hard Spanish cheese
4 tbsp extra virgin olive oil
crusty bread, to serve

For the salsa
200g (7oz) Home-preserved
   chopped tomatoes (page 32)
   or a 200g (7oz) tin of chopped
   tomatoes
2–3 guindilla peppers, chopped
1 small red onion, chopped
1 garlic clove, crushed
2 sprigs of oregano, leaves stripped,
   plus extra to garnish
2 tbsp sherry vinegar
1 tbsp extra virgin olive oil
flaky sea salt and freshly ground
   black pepper

First, make the salsa. In a bowl, mix together the tomatoes, guindilla, onion, garlic, oregano, vinegar and extra virgin olive oil and season to taste with salt and pepper.

On a large platter, arrange the heirloom tomatoes with the sun-blushed tomatoes. Spoon over the salsa.

Scatter with basil and payoyo shavings and drizzle with plenty of extra virgin olive oil before serving with lots of crusty bread.

Tip

This salad can be elevated by adding a very large handful of basil leaves and 120g (4oz) shavings of payoyo or other hard Spanish cheese.

Fermented spiced Spanish ketchup

- Makes 250g (9oz)
- Takes 15 minutes plus resting

It's time to elevate your condiment collection with my homemade ketchup recipe – with a Spanish twist, of course. Infused with the smoky essence of pimentón de la Vera, this delicious ketchup is, in fact, less of a simple ketchup and more of a gourmet sauce. The secret lies in its short fermentation period, which deepens the flavour, adding layers of flavour complexity that store-bought versions just can't match. This ketchup is a revelation, enhancing anything from fries to meats and everything in between.

For a pairing from heaven, try it with the Lolo de ternera sandwich (page 52). While the pineapple ketchup served at the restaurant Lolo, in Bermondsey Street, leans towards the sweeter side, this recipe offers a smokiness and depth that complements a wide range of produce.

225g (8oz) tomato purée (paste)
2 tbsp maple syrup
3 tbsp raw vinegar
3 tbsp brine from sauerkraut, whey from live yoghurt or water kefir
2 tsp sweet smoked pimentón
flaky sea salt and freshly ground black pepper

Mix all the ingredients together, adjusting the seasoning with salt and pepper to taste. Loosen with a few drops of water, if needed.

Spoon into a sterilised (page 32) Kilner (Mason) jar with an air lock. Close the jar (without sealing fully) and leave to stand at room temperature for 2–3 days, then seal and transfer to the fridge for at least another 3 days before using.

The Spanish Pantry

Pan con tomate verde

- Serves 2–4
- Takes 15 minutes

This recipe offers a fabulous twist on the traditional tomato bread, infusing it with the green perkiness of unripe tomatoes. Reflecting on this dish, I'm reminded of the film *Fried Green Tomatoes at the Whistle Stop Café*. Interestingly, fried green tomatoes weren't actually typical in Southern American cooking until they were popularised by the film – but then became a classic across the South! My version is delicious on its own or it goes remarkably well with top-quality tinned sardines.

When paired with a glass of Txakoli, the flavours sing. The wine's crispness beautifully complements the acidity of the tomatoes and the spice from the guindillas.

3 medium green heirloom tomatoes (about 200g (7oz))
2 guindilla peppers, finely chopped
4 small ciabatta or white rolls split in half
1 tbsp olive oil
1 garlic clove
3 tbsp extra virgin olive oil, plus extra to serve
flaky sea salt and freshly ground black pepper

Grate the tomatoes into a bowl, then add the guindilla and plenty of salt and pepper.

Brush the bread with the olive oil on both sides. Heat a pan over a medium–high heat and toast on both sides until golden. Remove from the pan and rub one of the sides with the garlic. Drizzle with the extra virgin olive oil.

Spoon the green tomato mixture over the bread, drizzle with more extra virgin olive oil and serve.

The Spanish Pantry

Chilled roast tomato soup with figs

- Serves 4–6
- Takes 1½ hours plus chilling

This recipe is a story in a bowl for me, rich with the flavours of summer and brimming with nostalgia. While my mum's tomato soup involved frying tomatoes with onions and bread, my recipe takes a different path, exaggerating the natural sweetness of vine-ripened tomatoes by roasting them to intensify their flavour. The addition of figs – especially if you can find the Oñigal variety, a small, honey-sweet variety from Extremadura – transforms the soup into something really special.
We once had a fig tree in my dad's vegetable garden and the fruit from that tree paired beautifully with my mum's tomato soup, proving that life, indeed, is about savouring the memories we make.

2kg (4lb 8oz) ripe vine tomatoes
1 garlic bulb, cloves separated
good pinch of chilli flakes
olive oil, for drizzling
2 banana shallots, finely chopped
4 sprigs of oregano
1 litre (34fl oz/4 cups) fresh
    chicken stock
4 ripe figs
extra virgin olive oil, for drizzling
flaky sea salt and freshly ground
    black pepper

Preheat the oven to 150°C fan (170°C/340°F/gas 3).

Halve the tomatoes and put on baking trays cut-side up. Scatter with the garlic cloves and chilli flakes. Drizzle with lots of olive oil and season well with salt and pepper. Roast for 45 minutes–1 hour, swapping the trays halfway through, until lightly caramelised.

Heat a little more oil in a pan and gently fry the shallots for 10 minutes. Add the roasted tomatoes. Squeeze the insides of the roasted garlic into the pan, discarding the skins.

Add the oregano and pour over the stock. Bring to the boil, then simmer for 10 minutes. Remove from the heat and cool, then chill until you are ready to serve.

Quarter the figs and toss with some salt and a drizzle of extra virgin olive oil. Spoon the soup into bowls, top with the figs and another drizzle of extra virgin olive oil and some black pepper. Serve.

Green tomato mermelada
with grilled pork chops

- Serves 4 (makes
  4–6 × 375 g/1 lb jars
  of mermelada)
- Takes 1 ½ hours for
  mermelada and
  30 minutes plus
  marinating for the
  chops

My tomato jam has been popular in my restaurants since the opening of José in 2011, consistently joining our cheese selections with a unique blend of orange and cinnamon, which enrich the aroma and flavour. This version, featuring green tomatoes, marries the tangy sharpness of the fruit with the zestiness of citrus and a subtle warmth from the ginger.

4 × 200g (7oz) pork chops on the
    bone (or 2 × 500g (1lb 2oz) chops)
5 sprigs of thyme
3 garlic cloves, bashed
½ tsp sweet smoked pimentón
2 tbsp olive oil
flaky sea salt and freshly ground
    black pepper
green salad, to serve

For the mermelada
2 unwaxed navel oranges
1 unwaxed lemon
1kg (2lb 4oz) green tomatoes
1kg (2lb 4oz/5 cups) preserving sugar
750ml (26fl oz/generous 3 cups) water
1 piece stem ginger in syrup, finely
    chopped

Tips

You can buy pork chops from Ibérico pigs easily online. Of course, you can make the *mermelada* well in advance.

Setting point is 104°C (220°F) on a sugar thermometer but you can test by keeping a couple of small plates in the freezer. When you think the preserve has reached setting point, spoon a little onto a chilled plate and push with your finger. If it wrinkles, then it is ready. If not, boil for another couple of minutes and test again.

Start with the *mermelada*. Pare the zest from the oranges and lemon and finely shred. Put the shredded zest into a small pan, just cover with water and bring to the boil, then simmer for 5 minutes. Drain.

Meanwhile, remove the pith from the fruit, chop the flesh and put it into a large preserving pan. Put the pips into a muslin pouch and set aside.

Chop the green tomatoes and add to the preserving pan with the sugar. Stir well and leave to macerate for at least 3 hours, stirring occasionally.

Add the water, the little bag of pips and the shredded zest and heat gently to make sure the sugar has totally dissolved, stirring occasionally.

Bring to a rolling boil and boil hard until you have reached the setting point (see Tips). Discard the bag of pips, stir in the stem ginger, then pour the marmalade into sterilised jars (page 32). Seal and label.

Put the chops into a large dish and add the thyme, garlic, pimentón and oil. Season well with salt and pepper and marinate for at least 30 minutes.

Preheat the oven to 180°C fan (200°C/400°F/gas 6).

Heat a heavy-based ovenproof pan or griddle pan to hot and sear the chops all over for 2–3 minutes on each side until golden. Then transfer to the oven and cook for 15 minutes until just cooked but still very juicy. Serve with the mermelada and a green salad.

Pisto-stuffed tomatoes

- Serves 6
- Takes 1 hour

This stunning dish is my ode to summer vegetables, capturing the essence of the season. Traditionally, my *pisto* (ratatouille) recipe requires a few hours of very slow cooking to achieve the deepest caramelisation and a delightful mushy texture. However, this quicker version doesn't skimp on flavour; a stint in the oven allows the vegetables to meld perfectly. There's something about this recipe that makes me happy, and warms my heart – maybe it's the charming, rustic style or the old-fashioned comfort it provides. Whatever the reason, it's nostalgic and rich, ideal for family gatherings or buffets.

It's particularly enjoyable with an ice-cold beer on a hot summer evening outdoors.

5 tbsp olive oil
1 medium aubergine (eggplant), diced
1 banana shallot, finely sliced
2 garlic cloves, bashed
1 courgette (zucchini), chopped
1 red (bell) pepper, chopped
200g (7oz) cherry tomatoes, halved
4 sprigs of oregano
finely grated zest of 1 lemon
2 tbsp sherry vinegar
6 beef tomatoes
4 tbsp extra virgin olive oil
lots of fresh basil leaves
salt and freshly ground black pepper

Heat the olive oil in a sauté pan or shallow casserole and fry the aubergine for 10 minutes, turning occasionally until they are lightly coloured and have released the oil back into the pan.

Add the shallot and fry for 5 minutes until softened, then add the garlic, courgette and pepper. Fry for 5 minutes, before adding the cherry tomatoes, oregano, lemon zest and vinegar, and stir to combine.

Cut the top off the beef tomatoes and scoop out the insides. Chop these scooped-out bits and add to the pisto. Season well with salt and pepper and simmer gently for 15–20 minutes; the tomatoes will relax and soften, creating the juice.

Preheat the oven to 160°C fan (180°C/350°F/gas 4).

Spoon the pisto into the tomatoes. Drizzle with some of the extra virgin olive oil and bake for 15 minutes, then serve with a good scattering of basil leaves and some extra virgin olive oil.

Tomato-cured sea bass and cockles

- Serves 4
- Takes 1 hour

When prepared in this way, these tomatoes are pure candy: sweet and succulent. Roasted low and slow, they provide a stunning contrast to the fresh, delicate fish, while the cockles contribute a delightful burst of seaside flavour. Finished with a squeeze of lemon and a sprinkle of fresh basil, this light yet richly flavoured dish serves as the perfect sharing plate that I promise will impress your guests.

300g (10½oz) cherry tomatoes
2 tbsp olive oil
600g (1lb 5oz) very fresh, line-caught wild sea bass fillets
125g (4oz) tinned or smoked cockles
juice of 1 lemon
lots of fresh basil leaves or micro herbs
flaky sea salt and freshly ground black pepper

Preheat the oven to 130°C fan (150°C/300°F/gas 2). Halve the tomatoes and put on a baking sheet cut-side up. Season with salt and pepper and drizzle with oil. Roast for 35–40 minutes until starting to become sticky. Set aside.

Finely slice the sea bass, arrange on a platter and scatter with the cockles. Press half the cherry tomatoes through a sieve and mix the juices with the lemon juice and plenty of seasoning. Scatter the rest of the tomatoes over the fish, then drizzle with the juices. Scatter with the basil or herbs and serve immediately.

Peppers

Peppers, one of Spain's favourite ingredients, hold a special place in Spanish cuisine, both for their distinctive flavour and their historic journey to Spain. As with tomatoes, when Columbus returned from the Americas in the late 15th century, he presented peppers as a gift to the Catholic monarchs, Queen Isabella and King Ferdinand. They were considered to be exotic fruits and intrigued the Spanish court. Very quickly they found a natural home in Spain's warm climate, where they became a key part of our culinary traditions.

One of the most iconic contributions to Spanish cuisine from peppers is pimentón de la Vera, a smoked paprika originating in La Vera, Extremadura. Monks in my home region pioneered the production process, drying peppers by hanging them over oak fires, allowing the smoke to slowly infuse each one. This traditional method produces the distinctively rich, smoky flavour of pimentón, available in sweet, bittersweet and spicy varieties. Today, it's an essential seasoning in a lot of Spanish cooking, adding exquisite depth to dishes like stews, rice dishes, seafood dishes and, of course, chorizo.

Fresh peppers are equally celebrated in Spanish kitchens. A firm favourite is padrón peppers, now a classic tapa. These small, green peppers are rapidly blistered in hot oil, then sprinkled with coarse salt, creating a simply irresistible dish with a fun element of surprise – most are mild, but occasionally you'll bite into a spicy one! It's good luck.

Another well-loved dish is Peppers stuffed with slow-cooked ragu (page 61) – *pimientos rellenos* – filled with seafood, minced meat or a creamy béchamel to bring out the natural sweetness of the pepper. From royal courts to local kitchens, peppers have certainly taken root in Spanish culinary culture. Whether it's the smoky warmth of pimentón de la Vera or the fresh sweetness of roasted peppers, these flavours are now indicative of Spanish cooking.

Lolo de ternera sandwich

- Serves 2
- Takes 30 minutes

The *pepito de ternera* is a sandwich loved throughout Spain, with a special place in Madrid's culinary scene. Its origins are a bit of a mystery, but one popular story says it all began with a man named Pepito who wanted something simple and hearty so he asked his local bartender for a quick sandwich made with freshly cooked beef. What started as his personal request soon became a hit, earning its place on menus and being named after its original fan.

While the ingredients can vary, what you'll almost always find is a crusty bread roll, tender beef and, in many cases, green peppers. These simple elements are what make the *pepito* so iconic: straightforward yet full of flavour.

At Lolo restaurant, we've taken this great classic and given it our own twist to create the *Lolo de ternera*. We've kept the essence of the original, with simple, satisfying and delicious flavours, but added a little flair to make it stand out. If you're feeling adventurous, there's an optional ketchup addition waiting for you (page 38).

2 green (bell) peppers
3 tbsp olive oil
2 garlic cloves, finely sliced
finely grated zest of 1 lemon
good pinch of chilli flakes
300g (10½oz) bavette steak
2 small ciabatta or small baguettes
75g (2½oz) Mahon or other melty
   cheese, sliced
2–3 tbsp fresh alioli or mayonnaise
flaky sea salt and freshly ground
   black pepper

Heat the grill to high and blacken the peppers all over, then pop them in a bowl and cover with clingfilm (plastic wrap). Leave until cool enough to peel. Peel and discard the seeds and skin, then tear the flesh into pieces.

Heat 2 tablespoons of the oil in a pan and fry the garlic, lemon zest and chilli for 1 minute, then add the peppers and toss together. Season with salt and pepper and set aside.

Season the steak with salt and pepper and drizzle with the remaining tablespoon of oil. Heat a heavy-based pan over a high heat and sear the steak for 2–3 minutes on each side until dark golden brown but still just pink inside. Allow to rest on a warm plate.

Split the bread in half and toast in the pan. Spoon the peppers onto the bottom slice of the bread, top with the cheese and pop under the grill just to melt.

Slice the steak and place on top of the melting cheesy peppers. Spread the top bun with alioli, add the steak and serve.

Tuna escabeche

- Serves 2–4
- Takes 30 minutes plus overnight marinating

This recipe is already a favourite of our friends and guests in Iris. I am truly proud to say that the bluefin tuna caught in the Cadiz-Barbate area is among the finest in the world. It is heartening to see that when we care for our world, diminishing food sources can return to healthy numbers. Governments must protect nature and, in turn, nature will heal. An example of how we can do this is evident with the bluefin tuna: since the government restricted the quantities and sizes that could be caught, the fish population rapidly recovered. This demonstrates that it is within our power to make ethical, sustainable decisions that look after our world properly. The quality of tuna fished using ancient methods in the Atlantic waters of Andalusia is second to none.

I recommend pairing with a rich wine such as Verdejo or Alavariño, that can cope with the acidity of the vinegar, wine, herbs and spices. Alternatively, it will match very well with a fino sherry en rama or a manzanilla, both really cold.

2 × 250g (9oz) tuna steaks
100ml (3½fl oz/scant ½ cup) olive oil
1 onion, finely sliced
2 red peppers, deseeded and thinly sliced
4 garlic cloves, finely sliced
1 red chilli, halved
2 bay leaves
5 sprigs of thyme
5 sprigs of marjoram
1 tsp black peppercorns
1 tsp cumin seeds
2 tsp coriander seeds
200ml (7fl oz/scant 1 cup) white wine
200ml (7fl oz/scant 1 cup) white wine vinegar
100ml (3½fl oz/scant ½ cup) water
3 tbsp extra virgin olive oil
flaky sea salt and freshly ground black pepper

Season the tuna steaks with salt and pepper and brush with a little of the olive oil. Heat a large, heavy-based pan over a high heat and sear the tuna for 2 minutes on each side until deep golden brown but still very pink in the middle. Set aside.

Reduce the heat of the pan a little and add the rest of the olive oil and the onion, red peppers, garlic and chilli and fry for a couple of minutes until fragrant. Add the herbs and spices and cook for a minute more, then add the wine, vinegar and water. Bring to the boil, then turn down the heat to a vigorous simmer until reduced by half.

Allow to cool to room temperature, then gently add the tuna to the escabeche and marinate in the fridge overnight.

Slice the steaks and serve with some of the pickling juices spooned over and a good drizzle of extra virgin olive oil.

The Spanish Pantry

Morcilla and piquillo hash

- Serves 4
- Takes 45 minutes

For the ideal breakfast, I always turn to the robust flavours of rural Spanish cooking. In this recipe, combining piquillo peppers, morcilla de Burgos, fried potatoes and eggs is a classic example. In this recipe I'm using morcilla de cebolla – a type of onion black pudding that's softer and more moist than other types, cherished throughout Spain for its delicate texture and depth of flavour. My absolute favourite morcilla is from Guadalupe in Extremadura, notable for a subtle spiciness that sets it apart.

When enjoying it for lunch or dinner, I recommend a glass of fresh, medium-bodied Mencía, to complement the rich, smoky notes of the dish.

600g (1lb 5oz) new potatoes
75ml (2½fl oz/scant ⅓ cup) olive oil,
   plus extra for frying
250g (9oz) morcilla
3–4 piquillo peppers, drained, patted
   dry and finely sliced
handful of flat-leaf parsley, chopped
4 free-range eggs
flaky sea salt and freshly ground
   black pepper

Put the potatoes in a pan of cold, salted water and bring to the boil. Simmer for 15 minutes until just tender. Drain.

Heat 1 tablespoon of the oil in a non-stick frying pan (skillet) and fry the morcilla for 5–6 minutes until golden brown and crisp on both sides. Remove from the pan and set aside.

Heat the rest of the oil in the pan and add the potatoes, squashing them down so they break open. Fry for 15–20 minutes until they are golden and crisp, then return the morcilla to the pan and toss together. Add the peppers and parsley to the pan and toss with plenty of salt and pepper. Stir in the parsley.

Heat a layer of oil in a non-stick pan and fry the eggs until the whites are set and the yolks runny.

Serve the hash with the eggs on top and sprinkled with plenty of pepper.

Pinchos moruno with romesco

- Serves 4
- Takes 50 minutes

This is one of our most popular tapa at José in Bermondsey, and always a crowd-pleaser at events. Some might think that using cheaper chicken would work just as well, assuming the flavours won't show the difference but that couldn't be further from the truth. The spices and other ingredients really bring out the delicate aspects of a high-quality chicken, so buy the best you can.

500g (1lb 2oz) free-range boneless chicken thighs, diced

For the marinade
2 garlic cloves, crushed
2 tsp cumin seeds
2 tsp smoked sweet pimentón
3 sprigs of oregano, leaves stripped
3 sprigs of thyme, leaves stripped
2 tsp sherry vinegar
2 tbsp olive oil

For the romesco
200g (7oz) ripe San Marzano tomatoes, cut into quarters
2 red (bell) peppers, deseeded and quartered
olive oil, for drizzling
30g (1oz/¼ cup) blanched hazelnuts
20g (¾oz) stale white bread, torn into pieces
1 garlic clove
2 tsp ñora paste
2 tsp Pedro Ximénez sherry vinegar
3 tbsp extra virgin olive oil
flaky sea salt and freshly ground black pepper

Tip

You could use a little smoked sweet pimentón if you don't have ñora paste.

Swap the pimentón for a hot version or add some chilli flakes if you fancy more heat!

Put the chicken in a bowl. Mix the marinade ingredients together and pour over the chicken, then leave to marinate while you make the romesco. Meanwhile, soak some wooden skewers in water.

To make the romesco sauce, preheat the oven to 200°C fan (220°C/425°F/gas 7).

Put the tomatoes and peppers in a roasting pan, drizzle with olive oil and season well with salt and pepper, then toss together to coat. Roast for 30 minutes.

Put the peppers into a bowl and, cover with clingfilm (plastic wrap) and steam until cool enough to handle, then peel off and discard the skins.

Heat a glug of oil over a medium heat and fry the nuts for 2–3 minutes until golden brown. Scoop out with a slotted spoon and set aside.

Add the bread to the pan and fry for a few minutes until golden brown, then add the garlic, tomatoes, peppers, ñora paste and sherry vinegar and fry for 1–2 minutes, stirring until well mixed.

Add the 3 tablespoons of oil and process in a food processor or use a stick blender to blend until almost smooth but still with a little texture.

Thread the chicken onto the soaked wooden skewers. Heat a griddle pan or heavy-based frying pan (skillet) over a high heat and sear the chicken all over until browned, then continue to cook until tender and cooked through. Serve with the romesco sauce.

The Spanish Pantry

Peppers stuffed with slow-cooked ragu

- Serves 8
- Takes 2 hours 40 minutes

Stuffed piquillo peppers have always been a popular dish in traditional restaurants and homes across Spain, often being filled with oxtail or bacalao. When these ingredients are a bit more difficult to find, you can create the same comforting experience with this recipe. While the flavours obviously differ, it maintains the essence of the classic dish while being a bit more accessible, making it perfect for home cooking.

Enjoy it with a lovely glass of Bobal, a grape variety common in Valencia and Utiel-Requena. Its richness will beautifully complement the bold flavours of this dish.

3 tbsp olive oil, plus extra for drizzling
1 large onion, finely chopped
2 celery stalks, finely chopped
2 garlic cloves, crushed
200g (7oz) cooking chorizo, skin removed and meat finely chopped
500g (1lb 2oz) minced (ground) pork
1 star anise
finely grated zest of 1 lemon
200ml (7fl oz/scant 1 cup) white wine
400g (14oz) Home-preserved chopped tomatoes (page 32) or 400g (14oz) tin of tomatoes
2 tbsp tomato purée (paste)
350ml (12¼fl oz/1½ cups) chicken stock
8 large green (bell) peppers
flaky sea salt and freshly ground black pepper

Heat the olive oil in a large sauté pan and gently fry the onion and celery for 10 minutes until really soft. Add the garlic and chorizo and cook for a further 5 minutes until the chorizo has released all of its oils.

Add the pork, increase the heat and brown all over, breaking it up with a spoon.

Add the star anise, lemon zest and white wine. Bubble for a few minutes.

Pour in the tomatoes, tomato purée and chicken stock. Season well with salt and pepper and bring to the boil, then reduce to a simmer and cook for 2–3 hours, stirring occasionally and adding a splash more water or stock if it starts to reduce too far.

Thirty minutes before you want to serve, preheat the oven to 180°C fan (200°C/400°F/gas 6).

Cut the tops off the peppers and deseed them. Place them in a roasting tin so they fit quite snugly. Drizzle with olive oil and season well with salt and pepper. Roast for 15–20 minutes until softened but still holding their shape.

Fill with the ragu and roast them for a further 15 minutes.

Tip

You can make the ragu in advance and freeze, then defrost and pick up the recipe at the penultimate paragraph of the method.

Gilda's devilled eggs

- Serves 4–8
- Takes 30 minutes

Back to the 1970s with devilled eggs! At Lolo, our Gilda features gordal olives – fat, juicy and beautiful – along with guindillas and the best, largest Catalina Gran Reserva anchovies. It's a Gilda that can't fit in your mouth all at once! In this recipe, we use smaller manzanilla olives, finely chopped guindillas and petite anchovies that are sweet and bite-sized, perfect for popping in your mouth – plus they look fantastic on top of a devilled egg.

The name for this *pintxo* actually comes from the 1946 film *Gilda* starring Rita Hayworth. This one was named after her because, just like Rita's character, it's spicy, a little salty, and quite a bit cheeky too.

I love all kinds of devilled eggs, and we serve them at Lolo with a variety of toppings, including smoked eel, sobrasada and anchovies. The alioli is blended right into the egg mixture, giving it a delicious base to elevate the flavour. Remember, the extra alioli keeps in the fridge for up to four days.

4 large free-range eggs
2 tbsp alioli (see below)
good pinch of smoked sweet pimentón, plus extra to serve
1 piquillo pepper, finely chopped
2 tsp capers, drained, rinsed and chopped
8 pitted manzanilla olives
8 small, salted anchovies
4 guindilla peppers, halved
extra virgin olive oil, for drizzling
flaky sea salt and freshly ground black or white pepper

For the alioli
2 free-range egg yolks
1 garlic clove, grated
1 tsp cider vinegar
200–250ml (7–8½fl oz/scant 1–1 cup) olive oil
2 tbsp extra virgin olive oil
1 tablespoon of just-boiled water
lemon juice, to taste

Put the eggs into a pan of cold water and bring to the boil, then boil for 6 minutes. Drain, then cool under cold running water.

To make the alioli, put the egg yolks in a bowl with some salt and pepper. Whisk in the garlic and cider vinegar.

Gradually whisk in the olive oil until you have a smooth, thick emulsion, then whisk in the extra virgin olive oil and 1 tablespoon of just-boiled water. Add lemon juice to taste and set aside.

Peel the eggs and halve them lengthways. Scoop the yolks out into a bowl and mash well, then add 2 tablespoons of the alioli, the pimentón, the piquillo pepper and the capers. Mix well, then spoon this mixture back into the egg white halves and arrange on a plate.

Thread 8 wooden skewers each with an olive, an anchovy and half a guindilla and place one on top of each of the eggs. Drizzle with extra virgin olive oil and serve.

Caramelised piquillo peppers with lamb cutlets

- Serves 4
- Takes 40 minutes

In Spain, our understanding of 'lamb' differs from many other countries in the northern hemisphere. We tend to eat lamb when it's very young, still suckling from its mother, hence calling it 'suckling lamb'. We use the sheep milk to make the world-famous Manchego cheese. I love this meat so much, and could easily devour a kilo by myself!

These days, it's definitely easier to find high-quality younger lamb in the UK; one of my favourites to cook and eat is Welsh salt-marsh lamb. It's always at the top of my list and brings back warm memories of those Sunday roasts with Hilda, Peter's mum, who knew how to cook it perfectly, served with her fresh mint sauce, and always such crispy roasted, delicious Welsh potatoes.

Piquillo peppers, on the other hand, come from Navarra in northern Spain. They're not very large or fleshy, but they have a beautiful smoky flavour, as they're roasted over charcoal. You'll usually find them in tins or jars. They're great as a garnish when grilled or, in this case, caramelised to create extra sweetness.

2 × 230g (8oz) jars of piquillo peppers
60g (2oz/heaped ⅓ cup) light soft brown sugar
finely grated zest and juice of 1 orange
1 bay leaf
3 garlic cloves, whole
3 tbsp olive oil
100g (3½oz) stale bread, torn into little pieces
2 × racks of lamb cutlets, divided into chops
2 tsp smoked pimentón
flaky sea salt and freshly ground black pepper

Drain the piquillo peppers, reserving the juice, and discard the seeds. Slice them and place in a pan with the juice, sugar, orange juice, bay leaf and garlic. Season with salt and pepper and cook gently for 20–25 minutes until they are deep brown and sticky.

To make the migas, heat a pan with 2 tablespoons of the oil over a medium–high heat and fry the bread until it is starting to become golden and crispy. Line a plate with paper towels. Add the orange zest and some sea salt to the pan and fry for a minute more, then tip the mixture onto the prepared plate.

Coat the lamb cutlets with the remaining olive oil, the pimentón and plenty of salt and pepper.

Heat the pan over a high heat and sear the lamb for 2–3 minutes on each side until deeply golden brown but still pink in the middle. Leave to rest for 5 minutes, then serve with the caramelised peppers and migas.

Green pepper and sardine empanada

- Makes 6
- Takes 1 hour plus chilling and resting

Empanadas should be more popular than they are! I wonder if people tend to think of pasties that are larger, made with shortcrust pastry that's often high in saturated fats, filled with starchy vegetables, and often mass-produced containing additives and high in salt. Empanadas offer a versatile and healthier option. They're made with a lighter, thinner dough, mostly baked, with a crispier texture and less fat. They're typically smaller and use a variety of lighter tasty fillings including vegetarian, vegan and some internationally inspired alternatives.

These ones are made with fresh sardines, but tinned sardines or even mussels work just as well. I recommend enjoying this dish with a glass of cold Albariño or a crisp, cold beer.

2 tbsp olive oil
2 banana shallots, finely sliced
4 green peppers (long ones if you can find them), deseeded and sliced
½ tsp chilli flakes
1 bay leaf
4 sprigs of thyme, leaves stripped
2 tbsp Pedro Ximénez sherry vinegar
12 tinned sardine fillets
flaky sea salt and freshly ground black pepper

For the pastry
250g (9oz/2 cups) plain (all-purpose) flour
½ tsp fine salt
100g (3½oz) cold unsalted butter, cubed
1 egg, beaten
2 tbsp cold water
1 tsp white wine vinegar

Heat the oil in a pan and fry the shallots for 5 minutes. Add the peppers, chilli flakes, bay leaf and thyme. Season with salt and pepper and cook for 30 minutes until lovely and soft. Add the vinegar and cook for a few more minutes, then leave to cool.

To make the pastry, tip the flour and salt into a bowl and rub in the cold butter with your fingertips until it resembles breadcrumbs. Mix half the beaten egg with the cold water and vinegar, add to the bowl and mix in quickly. Bring together with your hands and knead very briefly to make a smooth dough. Shape into a disc, wrap and chill for at least 30 minutes.

Preheat the oven to 180°C fan (200°C/400°F/gas 6) and line a baking sheet with baking parchment.

Divide the pastry into 6 even-sized pieces and roll into balls. Roll out into disc shapes and use a cutter or small plate to cut them into 16cm (6¼in) circles. Discard any trimmings.

Divide the pepper mixture between the discs, then top each one with 2 sardine fillets. Brush the edge with beaten egg, fold the pastry over the top of the filling and crimp the edges together.

Transfer to the prepared baking sheet and brush all over with beaten egg. Bake for 20–25 minutes until golden brown. Serve warm or at room temperature.

The Spanish Pantry

Braised oxtail with fried Padrón peppers

- Serves 4–6
- Takes 4 hours

Oxtail has a special place in my heart, ranking as one of my top-favourite meats. My most memorable experience of enjoying it was at Casa Morales in Seville. It was an experience that left an enduring memory and an indelible mark on my palate. The rich, gelatinous texture of the meat envelops the mouth and lips, creating a truly sumptuous experience. Paired with a glass of Palo Cortado and the fiery heat of freshly cooked Padrón peppers, it's a culinary explosion to accompany your best times. This recipe is designed to recapture the magic I experienced in Seville, combining the wholesome flavours of the oxtail with the robustness of the accompanying vegetables and the spirited kick of the peppers.

1.5kg (3lb 5oz) oxtail
50g (2oz/heaped ⅓ cup) plain (all-purpose) flour
100ml (3½fl oz/scant ½ cup) olive oil, plus extra to fry the peppers
1 large onion, finely sliced
1 carrot, diced
2 celery stalks, finely chopped
3 garlic cloves, bashed
3 sprigs of rosemary
300ml (10fl oz/1¼ cups) red wine
300ml (10fl oz/1¼ cups) fresh beef stock
250g (9oz) new potatoes
250g (9oz) Padrón peppers
flaky sea salt and freshly ground black pepper

Season the oxtail with salt and pepper and dust all over with the flour. Heat half the oil in a large, deep, flameproof casserole dish and brown the oxtail all over, in batches if necessary. Set aside.

Heat the rest of the oil in the dish and add the onion, carrot and celery and fry for 10 minutes until softened. Add the garlic and rosemary and cook for another minute, then add the red wine and bubble until reduced by about half.

Return the oxtail to the pan, add the stock and bring to the boil. Reduce to a simmer and cook, partially covered, for 3 hours until really tender and the sauce is lovely and thick, stirring occasionally and topping up with a little boiling water if needed.

Lift the oxtail from the pan and skim as much fat as you can from the sauce, then return the meat to the pan.

With a knife, break open the potatoes so they form a jagged edge, add to the casserole and cook for a final 30 minutes (remove the lid totally if it's still a bit saucy).

Next, in a large, heavy-based pan, heat a thin layer of oil, enough to cover the base of the pan, and fry the peppers until charred and tender. Season with salt and add them to the oxtail, then gently mix together before serving.

Chorizo

Chorizo is one of Spain's best-loved foods, easily recognisable by its deep red colour and smoky, savoury taste. Its roots go back centuries to when preserving meat was essential. Spaniards began curing pork with salt, garlic and other spices to make it last longer. Eventually, they added pimentón, which gave chorizo its iconic redness and signature smoky flavour. This brilliant combination of flavours turned chorizo into a Spanish classic.

As chorizo grew in popularity, each Spanish region adapted the recipe, infusing it with local flavours. In some areas, chorizo is notably spicier and smokier, while in others, it's distinctly milder or subtly sweet. Regional variations enhance Spain's rich culinary heritage. My favourite is always one made with pimentón de la Vera, because it's the magic ingredient in many of the best chorizo recipes, providing a distinctive flavour that sets this type of Spanish chorizo apart from many other high-quality sausages.

From its origins as a method of preserving pork to its ubiquity in every Spanish kitchen, chorizo has established itself as a true Spanish classic. Whether fried, grilled or stewed, chorizo delivers a bold, unmistakable flavour. Its smoky aroma envelops the kitchen when cooking with it, making it immediately recognisable and therefore a beloved addition to family meals and social gatherings, infusing each occasion with warmth and tradition.

Chorizo is extremely versatile in Spanish cooking, not only enjoyed on its own, although it's perfect when eaten as simply as that. Thinly sliced as a tapa, it pairs perfectly with cheese or olives, while in stews, it releases rich oils, adding depth and warmth. It's also delicious in rustic dishes like Chorizo and potato stew (page 75), where the sausage's smoky depth blends with the potatoes to create a hearty, satisfying meal. One of my favourite preparations is *Croquetas de chorizo* (page 74) and I have been asked so often for the recipe that I have included it here.

Tortilla vaga

- Serves 2
- Takes 20 minutes

The *tortilla vaga*, affectionately known as the 'lazy omelette', is a gorgeous food innovation that blurs the lines between an omelette and scrambled eggs. It has a pancake-like appearance but surprises with contrasting textures. It's perfectly cooked on one side while remaining luxuriously creamy on the other. This dish is a creation of Chef Sacha Hormaechea from Madrid, who envisioned an omelette that could offer the best of both worlds: the delicate firmness of a traditional omelette and the soft, rich scramble of eggs.

In his signature version, Chef Sacha tops the omelette with simple, flavourful ingredients: white butifarra sausage and piparras chillies, which add a gentle heat and a burst of flavour to the creamy base. My rendition of this recipe takes inspiration from his innovative approach while incorporating a personal twist to the toppings, adapting the dish to suit different tastes and occasions. Whether serving it for a leisurely brunch or as a quick, comforting meal, this delicious dish is a fine example of the simple pleasures of Spanish cooking.

75ml (2½fl oz/scant ⅓ cup) olive oil
150g (5oz) mixed mushrooms, torn or sliced
150g (5oz) cooking chorizo, chopped
4 free-range eggs
handful of soft herbs (parsley, chervil, chives), chopped
2 tbsp toasted pine nuts
extra virgin olive oil, for drizzling
flaky sea salt and freshly ground black pepper
toast, to serve

Heat 45ml (1½fl oz) of the olive oil in a frying pan (skillet) and fry the mushrooms over a high heat until golden and slightly crispy. Remove from the pan, drain on paper towels and season with salt. Add the chorizo to the pan and fry until golden brown, then scoop out with a slotted spoon and add to the mushrooms.

Beat the eggs with the herbs and plenty of salt and pepper, then tip into the pan. Cook over a low–medium heat, swirling loosely to help it set on the bottom. When it is almost set on the bottom but juicy and not quite set on the top, slide it out onto a plate, scatter with the toppings and pine nuts and serve with a good drizzle of extra virgin olive oil and toast.

Croquetas de chorizo

- Makes about 30
- Takes 1 hour, plus chilling

At long last, after many requests, I'm thrilled to share this recipe with you. This dish, loved for its simplicity and flavour, hinges on perfecting the béchamel sauce. Once you've mastered the velvety foundation, the world of croquetas is your oyster – you can more-or-less introduce any flavour you fancy. For this particular version, I've chosen a more intense mix of chorizo and chicken stock, which creates a rich, succulent depth to the béchamel.

If you fancy exploring other versions, consider using the aromatic soaking water from dried mushrooms for mushroom croquetas, or a good fish stock for an exquisite prawn version. The key to diversity lies in the béchamel; prepare it as outlined here, stir in your chosen ingredient, and continue with the same method.

There's nothing quite like enjoying these little bites of joy with a cold beer.

700ml (24fl oz/3 cups) whole milk
100g (3½oz) unsalted butter
125g (4oz/1 cup) plain (all-purpose) flour, plus 2 tbsp for dusting
200g (7oz) cured chorizo, finely chopped
4 sprigs of thyme, leaves stripped
125g (4oz) Manchego, grated
2 free-range eggs, beaten
150g (5oz/1 cup) panko breadcrumbs
1 litre (34fl oz/4 cups) light olive or vegetable oil, for deep-frying

Tip

If you want to keep these in the freezer for a later date, bring them out about an hour before you want to serve so they don't remain frozen in the centre when you cook them.

Heat the milk in a saucepan over a low heat. Melt the butter in a second pan, whisk in the flour and cook for 2–3 minutes.

Gradually whisk the warm milk into the butter and flour mixture with the stock, stirring, until you have a smooth, very thick sauce.

In a frying pan (skillet), gently fry the chorizo until golden and crisp. Add the thyme and cook for a further 1–2 minutes, then add this to the thick white sauce.

Line a baking sheet with clingfilm (plastic wrap), spread the sauce over the sheet and chill until cold.

Take spoonfuls of the mix and roll into balls about 30g (1oz) each. Put the 2 tablespoons of flour in a shallow dish and the beaten eggs and breadcrumbs in 2 more.

Coat each of the balls in flour, then beaten egg and finally breadcrumbs. Place on a baking sheet and, when they are all done, freeze for 1 hour.

When ready to cook, heat the olive or vegetable oil to 170°C (340°F). If you don't have a thermometer, a cube of bread will brown in 30 seconds. Drop a few of the croquetas into the oil and fry for 3–4 minutes until deep golden brown and hot to the middle. Remove with a slotted spoon and drain on paper towels while you fry the rest. Serve straight away.

Chorizo and potato stew

- Serves 4
- Takes 50 minutes

What could be more comforting on a chilly autumn day than a steaming bowl of stew? This hearty dish combines the smoky taste of chorizo with soft, creamy potatoes, tasty garlic and fragrant rosemary. It's a lovely mix that warms you up from the inside. With just a few simple ingredients and an easy recipe, this stew fills your kitchen with delicious smells and wraps you in a warm hug.

I love making this dish all year round, but there's something really special about enjoying it on a cool evening, definitely with a glass of manzanilla en rama.

4 tbsp olive oil
8 whole cooking chorizo sausages
1 red onion, finely sliced
6 garlic cloves, bashed
2 sprigs of rosemary
300g (10½oz) fresh tomatoes, roughly chopped
150ml (5fl oz/scant ⅔ cup) white wine
200ml (7fl oz/scant 1 cup) fresh chicken stock
300g (10½oz) smallish potatoes, peeled
handful of flat-leaf parsley, chopped
flaky sea salt and freshly ground black pepper

Heat the oil in a shallow, flameproof casserole dish over a medium–high heat and brown the chorizo sausages all over. Remove from the pan and set aside.

Add the onion to the dish and fry gently for 5 minutes, then add the garlic and rosemary and fry for a minute more until lovely and fragrant. Add the tomatoes and cook for 4–5 minutes, until starting to break down.

Add the white wine and bubble away for a few minutes, then add the chicken stock to the pan and return the chorizo. Season well with salt and pepper.

With the point of a knife, crack the potatoes open so they have jagged edges and add them to the dish. Bring to the boil, then reduce to a simmer and cook gently for 25–30 minutes until the potatoes have started to just break down and thicken the sauce. Scatter with parsley and serve.

The Spanish Pantry

Green bean and chorizo salad with egg ribbons

- Serves 4
- Takes 20 minutes

This recipe is undoubtedly one of my favourites; it's a simple yet intensely comforting meal, perfect for a midweek treat. Ready in just 20 minutes, it marries the smoky depth of cured chorizo with the crispness of fresh green beans and the delicate texture of soft egg ribbons. With only a handful of ingredients, this dish is straightforward to prepare yet rich in flavour.

Both at my mum's kitchen and my own, we often let the beans cook until they are exceptionally tender, enhancing their natural sweetness. A final dusting of pimentón de la Vera adds personality and a kick, elevating this dish to new heights of comfort food.

To perfectly round off this meal, I recommend pairing it with a glass of red Rioja Reserva to complement the rich flavours. Here's to a meal that is as satisfying as it is quick to prepare!

1 tbsp olive oil
200g (7oz) cooking chorizo, chopped
1 garlic clove, finely sliced
300g (10½oz) green beans, trimmed
2 free-range eggs, roughly beaten
smoked pimentón, for sprinkling
flaky sea salt and freshly ground
    black pepper

Heat the oil in a sauté or frying pan (skillet) and fry the chorizo for 5 minutes until golden. Add the garlic and fry for a minute more. Blanch the beans in a pan of boiling water, then drain.

Add the beans to the pan of chorizo and toss together.

Over a low heat, pour in the beaten eggs so it cooks in ribbons. Season with salt and pepper and serve with a sprinkle of pimentón.

Roast root veg with chorizo and bread

- Serves 2–4
- Takes 45 minutes

This dish is so unforgettable, I can't get it out of my mind; emerging from the oven bubbling and golden, filling the kitchen with irresistibly delicious aromas. The smoky chorizo is divine, and the chunks of sourdough bread eagerly absorb the rich, roasted flavours. It's an ideal choice for all sorts of get-togethers. Serve it piping hot, straight from the oven, topped with a sprinkle of fresh fennel leaves for an extra layer and hint of brightness. This beautiful, rustic creation is guaranteed to delight everyone at your table.

8 baby carrots, halved lengthways
3 baby or 1 large fennel bulb, cut into wedges
4 small beetroot (beets), halved or quartered
good pinch of smoked pimentón
2 tsp coriander seeds
2 tbsp olive oil
200g (7oz) cooking chorizo, skin removed and meat broken into pieces
200g (7oz) stale sourdough bread, torn into pieces
3 tbsp fresh chicken stock
large handful of fennel fronds or dill, chopped
flaky sea salt and freshly ground black pepper

Preheat the oven to 180°C fan (200°C/400°F/gas 6).

Tumble the veg into a roasting tin with the spices and oil. Season well with salt and pepper, then roast for 25 minutes, turning once.

Add the chorizo and mix together and return to the oven for 10 minutes.

Add the bread, tossing to coat in the chorizo oil, then drizzle with the chicken stock. Sprinkle with a little more salt and pepper and return to the oven for a further 10 minutes. Scatter with fennel fronds and serve.

The Spanish Pantry

Poached eggs with chorizo and broad beans

- Serves 2
- Takes 15 minutes

Nothing relaxes me more in the kitchen than shelling broad beans. It may sound odd, but it genuinely makes me happy – perhaps because I love them so much and know they'll soon be on the table. In Spain, you can find wonderful baby broad beans in shops, which are fantastic. Here in the UK, they're perhaps a bit harder to come by, but we do have great ones in season, and they're incredibly easy to preserve in jars (page 200).

1 tbsp olive oil
200g (7oz) cooking chorizo, skins removed, broken up
2 garlic cloves, finely sliced
1 tsp cumin seeds
200g (7oz) broad beans
2 free-range eggs
2 thick slices of bread
2 tbsp extra virgin olive oil
2 tbsp finely snipped chives
flaky sea salt and freshly ground black pepper

Heat the olive oil in a frying pan (skillet) and fry the chorizo over a medium heat until it is golden brown and crisp and has released its oils.

Add the garlic and cumin and fry for a minute. Add most of the beans to warm through. Season to taste with salt and pepper.

Poach the eggs in a pan of barely simmering water and toast the bread.

Drizzle the bread with the extra virgin olive oil and a little of the oil from the beans, then spoon the beans on top. Add an egg to each plate and scatter with chives to serve.

Tip

Instead of the braised broad beans, you can use 300g (10½oz) frozen baby broad beans and add some finely grated lemon zest.

　The Spanish Pantry

Patatas à la importancia con chorizo

- Serves 4
- Takes 45 minutes

The name of this dish translates to 'very important chorizo potatoes' and the original hails from Castilla y León, where the humble potato is elevated to star status through a simple yet elegant cooking technique. Traditionally, the potatoes are sliced, dipped in flour and egg and fried, then simmered in a flavourful broth. This version brings a spectacular twist with the addition of chorizo, infusing the dish with that magical, smoky depth.

My first encounter with this dish was at El Mesón de Doña Filo just outside Madrid, where I worked alongside my friends Julio and Imma. We prepared it without chorizo, using fish stock instead, and served it as a garnish for fish. Here, you can savour it in various ways: enjoy it as a hearty starter, a sharing dish, or as the perfect accompaniment to pork chops (page 44).

3 tbsp olive oil
120g (4oz) cured chorizo, sliced
pinch of saffron threads
1 tbsp just-boiled water
3 yukon gold or other semi-waxy
    potatoes (about 350g (12oz))
30g (2oz/¼ cup) plain (all-purpose)
    flour
pinch of pimentón
2 free-range eggs, beaten
1 large banana shallot, finely sliced
2 garlic cloves, finely sliced
120ml (4fl oz/½ cup) white wine
450ml (15¾fl oz/scant 2 cups) fresh
    chicken stock
handful of flat-leaf parsley, chopped
flaky sea salt and freshly ground
    black pepper

Heat the oil in a frying pan (skillet) and fry the chorizo over a medium heat until golden brown and starting to crisp. Scoop out with a slotted spoon and set aside.

Put the saffron threads in a small bowl and pour over the just-boiled water.

Peel and thickly slice the potatoes. Mix the flour with the pimentón and salt and pepper and dredge the potato slices in the flour, then in the beaten eggs.

Fry in batches for 1–2 minutes on each side until golden brown. Remove from the pan with tongs and set aside with the chorizo.

Add the shallot and garlic to the pan and fry for 5 minutes until softened, then stir in 1 tablespoon of the leftover flour and cook for 1–2 minutes, stirring continuously.

Add the saffron and its soaking water and the wine and bubble until it has reduced by half.

Add the stock to the pan, season with salt and pepper and return the potatoes and chorizo, spreading them out as much as possible. Simmer gently for 20–25 minutes until the potatoes are tender and most of the stock has been absorbed. Scatter with parsley and serve.

Chorizo corn dogs with sherry vinegar dipping glaze

- Makes 6
- Takes 45 minutes

This is a fun tapa and a perfect party food! A playful twist on the classic American corndog, chorizo corndogs bring Spanish personality to the popular snack. By replacing the usual sausage with spicy chorizo, these are packed with flavour and deliciousness. Pairing them with a sherry vinegar for dipping creates a great level of acidity that works well with the oils from the chorizo and frying.

Enjoy with any high-acidity wines like Albariño, Verdejo, Godello or a young cava. My choice would be a light, crisp cold beer.

150g (5oz/1 cup) fine cornmeal (or fine polenta)
50g (2oz/heaped ⅓ cup) plain (all-purpose) flour, plus extra for dusting
1 tsp caster (superfine) sugar
good pinch of mustard powder
½ tsp hot smoked pimentón
½ tsp baking powder
½ tsp sea salt
1 large free-range egg, lightly beaten
140ml (4½fl oz/generous ½ cup) whole milk
700ml (24fl oz/3 cups) olive oil, for frying
18 small, round, spicy cooking chorizo

For the glaze
75ml (2½fl oz/scant ⅓ cup) Pedro Ximénez sherry
2 tbsp Pedro Ximénez sherry vinegar
1 tbsp honey
1 tsp coriander seeds

Soak 6 wooden skewers in warm water for 30 minutes.

Mix the cornmeal, flour, sugar, mustard, pimentón, baking powder and salt in a bowl. Make a well in the middle and add the egg, then gradually whisk in the milk a little at a time and whisk until you have a smooth, thick batter.

Heat the oil in a wide, deep pan until it reaches 180°C (350°F). If you don't have a cooking thermometer, a cube of bread should brown in 25 seconds. Push 3 little chorizo onto each wooden skewer, leaving a small space in between them for the batter to go around. Dip the chorizo in the batter, making sure they are completely coated.

Fry them 2 at a time in the hot oil for 4–5 minutes until golden brown. Drain on paper towels, then repeat with the remaining sausages.

Meanwhile, heat the sherry, sherry vinegar, honey and coriander seeds in a pan together until syrupy. Pour into a little bowl.

Serve the chorizo corn dogs with the sherry glaze dip.

Manchego

Manchego cheese is one of Spain's most-loved foods, rooted in the history and landscape of La Mancha, the land of Don Quixote. Being made only from the milk of the Manchega sheep, it has been produced in the region for centuries, with records of its production going back to Roman times. The rich, nutty flavour comes from the unique diet of the sheep, grazing on the grasses and herbs of the rugged terrain.

In the past, Manchego was an integral part of rural life. Sheep were highly valued animals because they could survive the tough, dry climate of La Mancha, and their milk was a vital food source for families. To make the best cheese, lambs were often weaned early, so the sheep could return to milk production more quickly. This is also why lambs are eaten very young in the region, a tradition tied to the cheesemaking process.

In our home, my mum would make her own cheese with milk from our sheep and cows. She would collect the milk, curdle it, press it, then carefully age the cheese until it was ready. It wasn't fancy, but it was our family cheese, simple and full of flavour, and tied to the land and animals that sustained us. Helping her make it taught me so much about the pleasure of creating something from scratch, with care and patience.

Today, Manchego is enjoyed all over the world, but in Spain, it's a big deal. It's a part of our agricultural heritage, telling the story of how hard work, resourcefulness and respect for nature can create something truly special. Manchego connects us to our roots and, equally, to each other.

Manchego and anchovy spiced chicken escalopes

- Serves 4
- Takes 40 minutes

Chicken escalope is, of course, a family favourite, thanks to its versatility and ease of preparation. This dish is perfect for everything from a satisfying meal at home to a leisurely picnic in the countryside. What makes it truly special is how it can be enjoyed either hot or cold, making it ideal for any occasion.

In this recipe, we take the classic chicken escalope and weave in rich Manchego cheese and salty anchovies, adding a depth of flavour that is both bold and satisfying. The sprinkle of oregano gives the dish a fragrant aroma, enhancing the overall sensory experience. When accompanied by a simple tomato salad, the escalope is perfectly balanced, with the fresh tomatoes providing a crisp, refreshing contrast to the rich, savoury chicken.

Whether you have it with a slice of rustic crunchy bread, or a fresh, bitter-leaf salad, this dish is best served with a very cold beer. Perfect for a family dinner or as a star dish at your next outdoor gathering, this chicken escalope recipe will impress and satisfy.

4 small (or 2 large) free-range chicken breasts
8 salted anchovy fillets
4 sprigs of oregano, leaves stripped, plus 1 extra sprig to garnish
2 tbsp plain (all-purpose) flour
2 large free-range eggs, beaten
75g (2½oz/1½ cups) panko breadcrumbs
60g (2oz) Manchego, grated
4 tbsp olive oil
flaky sea salt and freshly ground black pepper
sliced tomatoes or a bitter leaf salad, to serve

Put the chicken breasts between 2 pieces of baking parchment and bash them with a rolling pin until they are about 5mm (¼in) thick. Press 2 anchovy fillets and some oregano leaves onto the top of each one.

Season the flour with salt and pepper, then dredge each of the fillets in the flour. Dip each one in the beaten egg. Mix the panko and Manchego together and coat the fillets all over.

Heat the oil in a large, non-stick frying pan (skillet) over a medium–high heat and fry the breaded fillets (in batches if necessary) for 3–4 minutes on each side until deep golden brown. Drain on paper towels and keep warm while you fry the others.

Slice, scatter with oregano and serve with sliced tomatoes or a bitter leaf salad.

The Spanish Pantry

Crispy fried Manchego salad

- Serves 4
- Takes 30 minutes

This recipe is inspired by my much-loved Fried gordal olives stuffed with Manchego, a big favourite at Pizarro restaurant. Here, the creamy, nutty Manchego is fried until perfectly golden and crisp, bringing a warm, savoury crunch to the salad. Paired with peppery rocket and the vibrant sweetness of fresh blood oranges, the result is a dish that is both refreshing and deeply comforting. A simple honey-mustard dressing ties everything together, adding a zesty punch that balances the sweet, savoury and tangy flavours in every bite. For the best experience, serve the cheese straight from the pan while it's still hot and melting. While it definitely shines in this salad, the fried Manchego also makes a fantastic tapa on its own, perfect for sharing or as an indulgent snack.

150g (5oz) rocket (arugula)
2 oranges (or blood oranges, when in season), segmented
250g (9oz) Manchego, cut into cubes
2 tbsp plain (all-purpose) flour
1 free-range egg, beaten
100g (3½oz/2 cups) panko breadcrumbs
300ml (10fl oz/1¼ cups) olive oil, for deep-frying
1 tbsp honey
1 tsp Dijon mustard
juice of ½ lemon
3–4 tbsp extra virgin olive oil
flaky sea salt and freshly ground black pepper

Put the rocket and orange segments in a large serving bowl.

Dust the Manchego cubes in flour. Dip in the beaten egg, then coat all over in panko.

Heat the olive oil in a small, deep pan to 170°C (340°F). Fry the cubes of cheese a few at a time until golden and crispy. Drain on paper towels.

Blend half the honey with the mustard, lemon juice, salt and pepper, then whisk in the extra virgin olive oil to form a dressing. Pour it over the leaves and toss together. Drizzle the rest of the honey over the cheese and scatter over the salad and serve straight away.

The Spanish Pantry

Garlic and Manchego coca

- Serves 4–8
- Takes 1 hour plus standing and resting

Coca, a cherished staple from the Mediterranean regions of Spain, is versatile and unique. This flatbread can range from sweet to savoury, adapting beautifully to a variety of toppings.

What sets this *coca* apart is the meticulous preparation of the dough, which can be frozen after shaping for later use, ensuring you have a base ready for whenever the mood strikes. Topped with a special blend of roasted garlic-infused olive oil and sprinkled with Manchego cheese, this *coca* is crisp and flavourful and pairs brilliantly with a cheese board or served as a standout snack on its own.

12g (⅓oz) fresh yeast or 7g (1 heaped tsp) dried
330ml (11¼fl oz/1½ cups) lukewarm water
pinch of caster sugar
500g (1lb 2oz/4 cups) plain (all-purpose) flour, plus extra for dusting
2 tbsp fine sea salt
75ml (2½fl oz/scant ⅓ cup) extra virgin olive oil
2 garlic bulbs, whole
1 tbsp olive oil
2 tbsp finely chopped flat-leaf parsley
2 tbsp polenta (cornmeal)
100g (3½oz) Manchego, grated
flaky sea salt

Tip

You can freeze the *coca* dough after you have shaped it into balls and then defrost and continue with the recipe.

Cream the yeast in a bowl with a little of the water and a pinch of sugar until smooth. Add three-quarters of the remaining water and leave to stand, covered, for 30 minutes until it starts to bubble.

Sift the flour and salt into the bowl of a stand mixer. Add the yeast water and 1 tablespoon of the extra virgin olive oil and knead with the dough hook for 5 minutes on a low speed, adding more of the water if it looks a little dry. Leave to stand for 10 minutes, then knead again for 5 minutes until smooth and elastic. Cover and leave to stand for 1 hour, or until doubled in size.

Meanwhile, preheat the oven to 140°C fan (160°C/320°F/gas 2–3).

Drizzle the garlic bulbs with the olive oil and roast for 45 minutes until very tender. Allow to cool, then squeeze the soft flesh from the bulbs and mix with the remaining extra virgin olive oil and the parsley.

Divide the dough into 4 equal portions, then roll out on a lightly floured surface into 30cm (12in) tongue-like shapes. Sprinkle 2 baking trays with the polenta, place the dough pieces on top, cover with a clean cloth and leave to stand in a warm place for 15 minutes.

Preheat the oven to 220°C fan (240°C/475°F/gas 9).

Spread the flatbreads with the garlic oil, sprinkle with salt and scatter with the Manchego. Bake for 12–15 minutes, until the bases are golden and crisp. Serve immediately.

Roast potatoes with Manchego and pepper crust

- Serves 4
- Takes 1 hour

Who doesn't love perfect roast potatoes? These are not only a household favourite but are also going to be a star attraction on the menu at The Swan Inn, Claygate. What makes our roast potatoes exceptional is the decadent, nutty flavour of Manchego cheese, which imparts a wonderful richness. This is well complemented by a touch of smoky warmth from the pimentón de la Vera, while the lemon zest and a drizzle of honey add unexpected bursts of freshness and sweetness. This is ideal for an outstanding Sunday roast or as a remarkable side at any meal. These potatoes really shine when served with a side of romesco sauce (page 58). Be prepared to have to make them a regular thing at your dining table!

3 tbsp olive oil
800g (1lb 12oz) potatoes, peeled and cut into small chunks
2 garlic cloves, grated
finely grated zest of 1 lemon
1 tbsp extra virgin olive oil
75g (2½oz) Manchego
pinch of pimentón de la Vera
½ tsp freshly ground black pepper
1 tbsp honey, for drizzling
flaky sea salt

Preheat the oven to 180°C fan (200°C/400°F/gas 6) and heat the olive oil in a roasting tin.

Put the potatoes in a frying pan (skillet) of cold salted water and bring to the boil, then simmer for 3–4 minutes. Drain and return to the pan over a low heat to dry and fluff up.

Tumble the potatoes into the hot oil, then roast for 45 minutes, turning once, until golden and crispy.

In a small bowl, mix the garlic, lemon zest and extra virgin olive oil. Toss into the roasted potatoes, then scatter all over with the Manchego, pimentón and black pepper. Return to the oven for a further 10 minutes until the cheese is golden.

Scoop into a bowl, season with salt and drizzle with the honey to serve.

Manchego

The Spanish Pantry

Griddled baby gem salad with Manchego mustard dressing

- Serves 4
- Takes 25 minutes

This is a long-standing favourite at Pizarro restaurant in London and José by Pizarro in Abu Dhabi. The baby gem lettuce gets a striking char from the griddle, the flavour of which goes perfectly with the creamy Manchego dressing. Crispy capers will add a flavour dimension as well as a satisfying crunch. If you're looking for an extra burst of flavour, a few good-quality anchovies on top make a great addition. This salad is quick to prepare and full of flavour, especially with such an incredible dressing. It's a perfect starter or accompaniment, and ideal if you're looking for something fresh and vibrant for your menu.

3 tbsp capers
75ml (2½fl oz/scant ⅓ cup) olive oil
2 tbsp sherry vinegar
1 tsp Dijon mustard
5 tbsp extra virgin olive oil, plus
 extra for drizzling
40g (1½oz) Manchego, grated,
 plus extra to serve
4 baby gem lettuce, halved
small handful of chives, snipped
flaky sea salt and freshly ground
 black pepper

Rinse the capers and pat them as dry as you can with paper towels. Heat the olive oil in a frying pan (skillet) and fry the capers until deeply crispy. Drain on paper towels.

Blend the vinegar and mustard with plenty of salt and pepper, then add the extra virgin olive oil to form a thick dressing. Stir in the Manchego.

Brush the lettuce with extra virgin olive oil and griddle on a high heat until lightly charred. Arrange on a plate, drizzle over the dressing and scatter with a little extra cheese and chives before serving.

Buñuelos de Manchego

- Makes 25
- Takes 45 minutes

The appeal of these *buñuelos* lies not only in their perfect texture – crisp on the outside and sumptuously soft and cheesy on the inside – but also in the way they transform simplicity into such pleasure. I think this recipe elevates the traditional Spanish treat with a particular blend of ingredients that ensures every *buñuelo* is a delightful treat.

For an even more enhanced flavour experience, I recommend serving them alongside a tangy green tomato salsa (page 44). This adds a fresh contrast that dances with the *buñuelos*, making them totally irresistible. Again, something ideal for social gatherings, *buñuelos* are best enjoyed hot and tend to disappear quickly, so be prepared to keep frying!

50g (2oz) unsalted butter
260ml (9¼fl oz/generous 1 cup) whole milk
good grating fresh nutmeg
pinch of hot smoked pimentón
100g (3½oz/heaped ¾ cup) plain (all-purpose) flour
good pinch of flaky sea salt
2 large free-range eggs, beaten
80g (3oz) Manchego, grated
600ml (20fl oz/2½ cups) olive oil, for deep-frying
flaky sea salt, to serve

Heat the butter and milk together gently in a saucepan with the nutmeg and pimentón until the butter has melted. Increase the heat until it is almost boiling.

Add all the flour in one go and quickly stir together over a low heat until you have a thick, smooth roux. Cook for a few minutes, stirring, then remove from the heat.

Add the salt and then the eggs, one at a time, beating after each one until the mixture is smooth and glossy. Add the cheese and mix well.

Heat the oil in a deep-sided, heavy-based pan to about 170°C (340°F). A few at a time, drop small teaspoons of the mixture (don't worry if they are uneven) into the hot oil and cook for 3–4 minutes until golden brown. Scoop out with a slotted spoon onto a plate lined with paper towels. Sprinkle with flaky sea salt and serve straight away.

Almonds

Almonds here are taking centre stage because they add a sensational texture to dishes and their subtle, nutty sweetness is compatible with so many other ingredients. Almonds have such a deliciously unique flavour and it's a bonus that they add texture to the Spanish classics, proving why they have been a treasured ingredient in our cuisine for centuries. A small amount can go a long way, enriching everything from savoury stews to sweet desserts.

Almonds have deep roots in Spanish history, brought to the Iberian Peninsula by the Phoenicians and later cultivated extensively by the Moors, who recognised that Spain's climate was ideal for almond groves. Today, almonds are grown widely across Spain, particularly in regions like Andalusia and Valencia, where the mild winters and warm summers yield almonds of exceptional quality. We have almond trees in my dad's vegetable garden, and I've always loved picking the almonds when they're still green, though people call me crazy for it! There's something about that green, delicately sweet taste that I can't resist. It's wonderful to have almonds all year round.

Among the varieties, Marcona almonds are my favourite. Likely originating from the Alicante region, these almonds are rounder, slightly sweeter and have a recognisably smooth, buttery texture. They add a soft, nutty flavour, with a hint of almond blossom, and a touch of earthiness, that makes a unique addition to both traditional dishes and modern recipes, making them a pleasure to cook with.

In Spanish kitchens, almonds have a special role, particularly in beloved dishes like Ajo blanco (page 113), a chilled almond and garlic soup, and turrón (page 111), a traditional Christmas-time nougat. The richness of almonds adds a unique depth to sauces, as in romesco (page 58), and a beautiful balance to sweets, like the famous *tarta de Santiago* – Warm olive oil and almond cake with preserved peaches (page 108) – an almond cake from Galicia, even though almond trees aren't common in that area.

Monkfish and potato stew with almond picada

- Serves 6
- Takes 40 minutes

This recipe is where my passion for cooking truly comes through, with a beautiful blend of textures and flavours that warm the soul. At the heart of the dish are tender chunks of monkfish and earthy, creamy potatoes, simmered together in a rich vegetable stock to create an amazing stew that's perfect for sharing, especially on a chilly evening. What stands out here is the picada, a traditional Catalan condiment made from a robust blend of nuts, garlic and sometimes bread. This quirky mixture not only adds a crunchy texture and a deep nutty flavour, but also thickens the sauce, enhancing the overall richness of the meal.

3 tbsp olive oil
1 large onion, finely sliced
2 garlic cloves, finely sliced
600g (1lb 5oz) potatoes, peeled and chopped
1 litre (34fl oz/4 cups) vegetable stock
1 bay leaf
2 sprigs of rosemary
1 tsp pimentón
750g (12lb 10oz) monkfish tail, cut into large chunks

For the picada
2 tbsp olive oil
1 thick slice of slightly stale sourdough
1 garlic clove, crushed
75g (2½oz/heaped ½ cup) blanched almonds
1 ripe tomato, chopped
1 tsp cumin seeds
flaky sea salt and freshly ground black pepper

Heat the oil in a flameproof casserole and gently fry the onion and garlic for 10 minutes until really soft and golden. Add the potatoes, stock, herbs and pimentón and cook for 15 minutes until the potatoes are tender.

Meanwhile, make the picada. Heat the oil in a pan and fry the bread for a few minutes until golden brown on both sides. Put the bread with the rest of the picada ingredients and plenty of salt and pepper in a food processor and blitz together to form a paste.

Cook the monkfish and potatoes for 5 minutes then add the picada and simmer together for 10 minutes until the fish is tender and the potatoes have broken down.

Spoon into shallow bowls and serve.

Almendrados

- Makes 35
- Takes 30 minutes

Almendrados are traditional Spanish almond cookies, profoundly linked to the country's culinary history. Especially popular in Andalusia during Christmastime and the holiday season, these treats are believed to have their origins in Spain's Moorish past, when almonds became a central ingredient in many Iberian desserts. With a recipe that has remained unchanged for centuries, almendrados reflect, for me, Spain's love for simple, natural flavours.

They are very easy to make, but the best ones, in my opinion, come from the nuns who bake them in the various convents across Spain. One of my favourites is from the Convento de las Hermanas Clarisas in Cáceres, where the delicate texture and flavour are unforgettable. If I'm honest, I fell a little bit in love with the experience of buying them there too: the mystery of the hidden voice and the nun behind the door that you can't see, add a special curiosity to create great memories.

225g (8oz/heaped 1⅔ cups) whole blanched almonds, plus extra to decorate
100g (3½oz/½ cup) granulated sugar, plus extra to sprinkle
2 large free-range eggs, separated
finely grated zest of 1 lemon
75g (2½oz/heaped ⅓ cup) caster (superfine) sugar
35 blanched almonds, to decorate

Blend the almonds with the granulated sugar in a food processor until really finely ground.

Beat the egg whites and caster sugar until they form soft peaks, then fold into the egg yolks and lemon zest followed by the almond mixture, to form a soft dough.

Preheat the oven to 160°C fan (180°C/350°F/gas 4). Line a baking sheet with baking parchment.

Pinch off pieces of dough and shape into small walnut-sized balls. Sprinkle a little granulated sugar in a shallow bowl, then roll the balls to coat in the caster sugar. Flatten them slightly onto the prepared baking sheet and press an almond into the top of each.

Bake for 8–10 minutes until just golden. Allow to cool completely before serving or storing for up to 10 days in an airtight container.

Salad with green almonds

- Serves 4
- Takes 30 minutes

Green almonds, a rarity that marks the arrival of spring, evoke fond memories of my childhood when I eagerly picked them, revelling in their crisp, fresh taste. If you happen to spot these seasonal gems, don't hesitate to try them! Their tender, slightly grassy flavour and crunchy texture make them an exceptional addition to any salad.

This recipe is a tribute to the unique taste of green almonds. It harnesses their distinctiveness to lift a simple salad into a celebration of spring. However, if you find yourself preparing this dish later in the summer when green almonds are no longer available, toasted flaked almonds make an excellent substitute, offering a similar crunch and a nutty depth.

For an easy and adaptable summer dish, this salad is perfect. If you want to vary the ingredients further, preserved broad beans can replace peas (page 200). This substitution not only adds a wonderful texture but also enriches the salad with a robust flavour, making it a great choice for enjoying the bright, fresh flavours of the season.

2 courgettes (zucchini), sliced into ribbons
300g (10½oz) fresh peas in pod
150g (5oz) fresh green almonds
juice of 1 lemon
200g (7oz) requesón (page 130) or other curd cheese, crumbled
handful of tarragon, leaves picked
3 tbsp extra virgin olive oil
flaky sea salt and freshly ground black pepper

Arrange the courgettes on a platter. Pod the peas and scatter over the courgettes.

Slice the almonds and toss with half the lemon juice, then scatter over the platter along with the requesón and tarragon.

Mix the remaining lemon juice with plenty of salt and pepper, then whisk in the extra virgin olive oil to form a dressing. Pour over the salad and serve.

Warm olive oil and almond cake with preserved peaches

- Serves 10
- Takes 1½ hours

Grown in the heart of Spain, Calanda peaches are celebrated worldwide for their sweetness and vibrant, intense yellow colour. My dad always had a fondness for peaches in syrup – a simple yet profoundly delightful dessert that I regretfully never had the chance to make for him myself. However, I carried his memory with me as I developed this recipe, one I believe would have made him immensely proud.

100ml (3½fl oz/scant ½ cup) really good extra virgin olive oil, plus a little exra to grease the cake tin
100g (3½oz/heaped ¾ cup) plain (all-purpose) flour
125g (4½oz/1¼ cups) ground almonds
good pinch of fine sea salt
2 tsp baking powder
finely grated zest of 1 lemon
3 large free-range eggs
200g (7oz/heaped 1 cup) caster (superfine) sugar
180g (6½oz) plain yoghurt
icing (confectioners') sugar, for dusting

For the peaches
4 large ripe peaches
juice of 1 lemon
2 sprigs of lemon thyme (or thyme)
200g (7oz/heaped 1 cup) caster (superfine) sugar
200ml (7fl oz/scant 1 cup) water

To prepare the peaches, make a cross in the bottom of each peach with a sharp knife. Bring a saucepan of water to the boil and have a bowl of iced water ready on the side. Plunge the peaches into the boiling water for 20 seconds, then remove and put into the iced water. Once cool, halve and remove the stones, then peel the skin from the peaches. Put the peaches into a bowl and toss with the lemon juice and lemon thyme.

Put the sugar and water into a small pan. Over a low heat, dissolve the sugar, then bubble until you have a light sugar syrup. Allow to cool for 20 minutes.

Put the peaches into a sterilised jar (page 32), then pour over the syrup to cover completely. Close the jar and stand it in a pan of boiling water for 30 minutes to seal.

Preheat the oven to 170°C fan (190°C/375°F/gas 5) and grease a 23cm (9in) loose-bottomed cake tin with a little olive oil and line with baking parchment.

Put all the dry ingredients in a bowl with the lemon zest and whisk to combine.

In a large bowl with a hand whisk or in a stand mixer, beat the eggs and sugar until really pale and doubled in volume. On a low speed, whisk in the yoghurt, then the extra virgin olive oil.

Fold the dry ingredients into the creamy mixture. Spoon into the tin and bake for 1 hour–1 hour 10 minutes – covering with a piece of foil if it starts to get too golden – until a skewer inserted into the middle comes out clean.

Leave to cool in the tin for 15 minutes, then transfer to a wire rack to cool a little more. Dust with icing sugar before serving with the peaches.

The Spanish Pantry

Soft almond and orange blossom turrón

- Serves 8–10
- Takes 40 minutes plus cooling

Turrón is one of Spain's oldest and most cherished sweets, with roots tracing back to the Moorish period when almonds and honey were first combined in Iberian desserts. Over centuries, it became a symbol of Spain's rich culinary heritage, with Jijona (Xixona) and Alicante emerging as the epicentres of its production.

This version, with soft almonds and orange blossom, offers a twist on traditional turrón. While it's most often associated with Christmas treats, turrón is far too delicious to save for a particular time of the year. Its sweet, nutty flavour and melt-in-the-mouth texture make it a little slice of Spanish heaven to enjoy any time of the year. Warning: if you make it for your sweet-toothed friends, they'll keep asking for it.

2 sheets of rice paper
1 tbsp olive oil
225g (8oz/heaped 1 cup) granulated sugar
140g (4½oz) clear honey
1½ tbsp liquid glucose
110ml (3¾fl oz/scant ½ cup) water
2 large free-range egg whites
250g (9oz/scant 2 cups) blanched almonds, toasted and roughly chopped
2 tsp orange blossom water

Tip

You can use a hand mixer for this recipe but it is a bit more tricky when it comes to whisking in the sugar syrup.

Line the bottom of a 16cm (6¼in) non-stick square tin with rice paper and grease the sides really well with the oil.

Put the sugar, honey, liquid glucose and water in a heavy-based saucepan and stir over a very low heat until the sugar has dissolved.

Once it has fully melted, turn up the heat and boil rapidly. When the boiling sugar reaches 115°C (240°F), whisk the egg whites in the bowl of a stand mixer until they form very soft peaks, then, slowly but steadily, whisking all the time, pour the hot sugar syrup into the whisked egg whites, making sure it doesn't touch the sides of the bowl or the beaters.

Once all the syrup has been added, keep whisking until the mixture is extremely thick. Using a spatula, scoop the mixture back into the pan and cook over a low heat, stirring constantly, until the mixture starts to thicken even more, come away from the sides as you stir and become a pale brown colour. You are looking for the moment when you can drop a little bit into a bowl of water and it forms a ball that is firm but you can still squeeze it with your fingers.

Add the nuts and orange blossom water.

Spoon the mix into the prepared tin, scraping it out with a spatula or metal spoon, then press a second piece of rice paper on top and flatten it out to about 1cm (¾in) thick. Put a board or sheet on top and weigh it down. Leave to cool completely before cutting into squares.

The Spanish Pantry

Ajo blanco with roasted grapes

- Serves 4–6
- Takes 45 minutes plus chilling

Ajo blanco is one of Spain's oldest dishes. It's made by blending almonds, garlic and bread into a creamy, flavourful soup. Garlic, one of the key ingredients, likely arrived in Spain with the Phoenicians, and the Romans helped make it a staple in Spanish cooking. Long before we fell in love with gazpacho, ajo blanco was the go-to dish for beating the Andalusian heat, with its simplicity and flavour making it perfect for the climate. It soon became a timeless favourite.

In this version, I've added roasted grapes for a contemporary twist, bringing sweetness and warmth to the nutty, chilled soup. To dress, traditionally fresh grapes are used, but I like to finish it with toasted flaked almonds for a little extra texture.

250g (9oz/scant ⅔ cup) blanched almonds
1 bunch of white or blush grapes
100ml (3½fl oz/scant ½ cup) extra virgin olive oil, plus extra for drizzling
3 garlic cloves, peeled
750ml (26fl oz/generous 3 cups) cold water
175g (6oz) stale bread
3 tbsp whole milk
1 tbsp sherry vinegar
handful of chives, snipped
flaky sea salt and freshly ground black pepper

Soak the almonds overnight in cold water, then drain.

Preheat the oven to 160°C fan (180°C/350°F/gas 4). Drizzle the grapes in a little extra virgin olive oil and roast for 30 minutes until tender and lightly golden.

Put the garlic and water in a blender and blitz together until smooth and creamy-looking. Soak the bread in the milk for a few minutes, then add to the blender and blitz again before adding the drained almonds, the vinegar and the 100ml (3½fl oz/scant ½ cup) of extra virgin olive oil. Season well with salt and pepper and blitz all together until smooth. Chill for at least 30 minutes.

Pour the soup into bowls, top with the grapes and chives as well as a good grating of black pepper and a drizzle of extra virgin olive oil.

Caramelised almonds
with dulce de leche semifreddo

- Serves 8
- Takes 45 minutes plus freezing

Semifreddo – which translates to 'half-frozen' – is a sumptuous dessert that emerged from Italy in the late 19th century. Its origins are intertwined with those of parfaits and other frozen desserts, but it carved out a niche for itself thanks to its delightfully light and airy texture. Something really appealing is that, unlike traditional ice cream, it doesn't require any special equipment to prepare.

Regrettably, we don't see this dish as often as we should, which is a true food-world oversight, given its simplicity and elegance. This version, in particular, demonstrates the dessert's understated charm. It's deliciously rich and creamy, infused with a deeply indulgent caramel flavour. However, the real star of the show is the caramelised almonds. The sweet crunch not only contrasts beautifully with the smoothness of the semifreddo, but elevates the entire dessert to a new level of sophistication.

6 free-range eggs, separated
225g (8oz) dulce de leche, plus extra for drizzling (optional)
2 tbsp Pedro Ximénez sherry
500ml (17fl oz/2 cups) double (heavy) cream

For the almonds
100g (3½oz/heaped ½ cup) caster (superfine) sugar
3 tbsp water
good pinch of ground cinnamon
150g (5oz/scant 1 cup) blanched almonds

Line a 1 litre (34fl oz/4 cup) loaf tin with clingfilm (plastic wrap) or baking parchment.

Put the egg yolks and dulce de leche in a bowl and place over a saucepan of barely simmering water. Whisk with an electric hand whisk until really pale and voluminous and holding a ribbon shape when you lift out the beaters. Whisk in the sherry.

In a clean bowl, whisk the egg whites until holding soft peaks. In a third bowl, lightly whip the cream until just holding its shape.

Fold the cream into the whisked egg yolks, then very gently fold in the egg whites. Spoon into the prepared loaf tin and freeze overnight.

To prepare the almonds, put the caster sugar, water and cinnamon in a pan and place over a low heat until the sugar has melted. Add the almonds, increase the heat and bubble, stirring, until you have a deep caramel coating all the almonds. Tip out onto the baking tray and cool before breaking up.

Serve slices of the semifreddo with the almonds scattered over the top and an extra drizzle of dulce de leche, if you like.

Rare sliced rib of beef with almond and tarragon salsa

- Serves 4
- Takes 30 minutes

This dish draws its inspiration from my fond memories working at Eyre Brothers Restaurant, where I first discovered the allure of aromatic tarragon. It was there that I was properly introduced to this distinctive herb, and it quickly rose to the top of my list of favourites. Tarragon, with its fresh, slightly aniseed flavour, is rarely used in Spanish cooking, yet it offers a fantastic twist with its light, peppery notes.

Here, I've reimagined the original tarragon salsa that captivated me at Eyre Brothers, enhancing it with flaked almonds to add a bit of crunch and nuttiness, expanding the sauce in an alternative flavour direction. This salsa goes perfectly with a beautifully marinated rib of beef, making the dish not only a salute to my past culinary experiences but also flying the flag for tarragon.

1 × rib of beef on the bone
(about 1.2kg (2lb 12oz))
3 garlic cloves, bashed
3 sprigs of tarragon
2 tbsp olive oil
flaky sea salt and freshly ground
black pepper

For the salsa
100g (3½oz/1¼ cups) flaked (slivered)
almonds
35g (1oz) flat-leaf parsley, chopped
15g (½oz) tarragon, chopped
2 plum tomatoes, chopped
2 guindilla peppers, chopped
1 garlic clove, chopped
5–6 tbsp extra virgin olive oil

Put the beef in a dish with the garlic, tarragon and oil and plenty of black pepper. Leave to marinate while you make the salsa.

Lightly toast the almonds in a dry frying pan (skillet) over a medium heat, then roughly chop and tip into a bowl. Add the rest of the salsa ingredients and mix well. Season to taste with salt and pepper.

Heat a large, heavy-based pan over a high heat and once it is really hot, add the steak. Sear for 3–4 minutes, then flip over and sear for the same on the other side. Then reduce the heat to medium–high and flip again and cook for a further 3–4 minutes more on each side so that it has had 6–7 minutes on each side in total.

Transfer to a board or plate and season with salt, then leave to rest for 5–10 minutes.

Slice the steak, arrange on a platter and spoon the salsa over the top to serve.

The Spanish Pantry

Mini chocolate-coated almond ice creams

- Makes 30
- Takes 1 hour plus chilling, churning and freezing

After a long, leisurely, sun-drenched lunch at our favourite Chiringuito Pescador in Zahara de Los Atunes, my team from London and I were completely full, lounging back contentedly after devouring a large majestic grilled lobster – it's the sort of meal that etches itself permanently in the memory. Still enjoying the sun, listening to the waves of the sea, we enjoyed the final touch of mini 'Magnums' and coffee. In that perfect moment, we had an idea to transform this little treat. And here we are, ready to share our inspired creation with you.

75g (2½oz/¾ cup) ground almonds
400ml (13fl oz/generous 1½ cups) whole milk
200ml (7fl oz/scant 1 cup) double (heavy) cream
1 vanilla pod, split
120g (4oz/⅔ cup) caster (superfine) sugar
3 large free-range egg yolks
250g (9oz) milk chocolate, broken into small pieces
50g (2oz) chopped toasted almonds

Tip

You can also use really good-quality ice cream, such as pistachio or hazelnut, instead of making your own.

Toast the ground almonds in a pan over a low heat until lightly browned. Line a baking tray with baking parchment.

Put the milk, cream, vanilla pod and half the sugar into a pan. Add the toasted almonds and bring gently almost to the boil, then set aside to infuse with the almonds.

Put the egg yolks and the rest of the sugar in a bowl and beat with an electric hand whisk until it is thick and voluminous. Pour in the almond cream mixture and combine well, then return to the pan over a low heat and cook, stirring, until you have a thick custard.

Strain into a clean bowl and cover with clingfilm (plastic wrap) so it is touching the surface. Once cool, you can chill for at least 1 hour, or overnight is best.

Pour the mixture into an ice cream machine and allow it to churn until you have a delicious ice cream.

Spoon into small ball-shaped silicone moulds (like one to make ball ice) and freeze for at least 3 hours. (For some moulds you may have to fill 2 sides of semi-circles and stick them together.) Alternatively, scoop small balls with a melon baller and freeze for an hour, then roll them into rounds with your hands and return to the freezer for a further 2 hours.

Melt the chocolate in a bowl over a pan of barely simmering water. Set aside.

Remove the frozen ice cream balls from their moulds and use a cocktail stick (toothpick) to dip them into the melted chocolate, then roll them in the nuts. Once hardened, return to the freezer on a lined tray until ready to serve.

The Spanish Pantry

Meatballs with almond sauce

- Serves 4
- Takes 40 minutes

These meatballs in almond sauce are my reinterpretation of the classic meatball dish, departing from the traditional tomato-based accompaniment. This is best made from finely ground Marcona almonds, renowned for their sweeter, richer flavour, transforming the dish into something extra special. To add a layer of crunch that contrasts with the velvety sauce, consider toasting some flaked almonds and sprinkling them on top before serving.

Perfect for enjoying with a loaf of crusty bread – the ideal vehicle for mopping up every drop of the almond sauce. Don't forget a generous side of crispy homemade fries, which complements the richness of the meatballs and sauce.

For the meatballs
250g (9oz) minced (ground) beef
250g (9oz) minced (ground) pork
1 banana shallot, finely chopped
2 garlic cloves, crushed
50g (2oz/heaped ¾ cup)
    breadcrumbs
75ml (2½fl oz/scant ⅓cup) whole milk
1 large free-range egg
good pinch of smoked pimentón
flaky sea salt and freshly ground
    black pepper
handful of chopped parsley, to
    garnish
30g (1oz/heaped ¼ cup) of toasted
    flaked almonds, to garnish

For the sauce
3 tbsp olive oil
1 garlic clove, finely sliced
100g (3½oz) slightly stale white bread
30g (1oz/heaped ¼ cup) ground
    almonds
½ tsp smoked pimentón
120ml (4fl oz/½ cup) white wine
1 tbsp sherry vinegar
500ml (17fl oz/2 cups) fresh
    chicken stock

First, make the meatballs. Put all the ingredients in a bowl and season generously with salt and pepper, then use your hands to squeeze and mix together thoroughly. Shape into about 20 small walnut-sized balls. Chill for 15 minutes.

Meanwhile, make the sauce. Heat the oil in a pan and gently fry the garlic for a minute, then add the bread and fry until lightly golden. Add the almonds and pimentón and fry for 1–2 minutes until the almonds are lightly toasted.

Add the wine and vinegar and bubble for a minute before adding the stock. Season well with salt and pepper, then add the meatballs to the sauce and bubble gently for 10–12 minutes until the sauce is reduced by about two-thirds and the meatballs are cooked through.

Scatter with the parsley and flaked almonds and serve.

Citrus fruits

Citrus fruits have been part of Spanish cuisine for centuries, ever since early Arab traders introduced oranges, lemons and limes in the 10th century. Regions like Valencia and Andalusia turned out to offer perfect climates for growing these fruits, and now Spanish citrus is famous worldwide for its lively, fresh flavours. Spanish oranges, with their intense sweetness, are especially prized, while lemons and limes add clean, bold flavours to traditional dishes.

In the kitchen, citrus fruits are incredibly adaptable, with each part of the fruit, from the zest to the juice, finding its purpose in all sorts of recipes. Preserved lemons are a fantastic way to add a deep, savoury citrus flavour to stews, roasted meats and slow-cooked dishes. Their intense flavours draw out the otherwise hidden notes in various hearty recipes, making them a favourite in my kitchen. Citrus also enhances sauces, marinades and salad dressings, establishing a freshness and characterful twist to nearly any dish.

We're lucky enough to have various citrus trees in my dad's garden, where the fruit is plentiful and grows plump and fragrant. There's nothing better than picking a sun-warmed orange or lemon straight from the branch, and this fresh juice and zest make a world of difference in cooking. When my dad saw the price of oranges and lemons in the UK, he was bemused, and not least due to their small size and sour acidity! After that visit he often told me he thought he should just bring a cargo of his own citrus fruits over from Spain. I had to laugh, but he's not wrong: there's something incredibly special about Spanish citrus, with their vibrancy, juiciness and aroma. It's this taste of home that inspires me to use citrus every chance I get, bringing a bit of Spanish sunshine into our food.

Olive oil-braised artichokes with lemon

- Makes 16 halves
- Takes 1½ hours

Artichokes are one of those ingredients I always love to cook with because they're so delicious and versatile. Whether preserved in jars for year-round use, fried as a stunning garnish as we do at José by Pizarro in Abu Dhabi, or simply sautéed with garlic and jamón, artichokes consistently deliver delightful flavours.

Lately, I've developed a preference for artichokes cooked al dente. While in Spain it's common to find jarred artichokes that are quite soft, and there's certainly a place for these in traditional dishes, I find that cooking them just until they're tender yet firm enhances their natural flavour and preserves their texture beautifully.

Artichokes have held a high-ranking place in Spanish cuisine for centuries – introduced by the Moors and now celebrated in regions like Andalusia and Catalonia. To me, they represent not just a piece of our history but a vibrant, indispensable component of modern cooking.

3 lemons
8 medium artichokes
125ml (4fl oz/½ cup) extra virgin
    olive oil
5 sprigs of thyme, leaves stripped
2 garlic cloves, crushed
2 tsp flaky sea salt

Tip

Use for salads, rice dishes, charcuterie and cheese boards or on toast with Manchego.

Keep one half of a lemon and pare the zest and squeeze the juice from the rest. This should yield about 130ml (4fl oz/½ cup) of lemon juice.

Preheat the oven to 170°C fan (190°C/375°F/gas 5).

Prepare the artichokes. Trim the stems, then snap off the tough outer leaves, pulling them away from the main globe until you see a colour change to a lighter pale green. Cut off the top one-third of the artichoke to remove the spines, then trim down to the heart with a paring knife, rubbing all the cut surfaces with the lemon half to stop them turning brown. Cut the heart in half and scrape out the feathery choke with a spoon. Cut each piece in half again.

In a frying pan (skillet), mix the lemon zest, juice, oil, thyme, garlic and salt, then add the prepared artichokes. Once they are all in the pan, bring to the boil over a high heat, then tip it all into a baking dish and cover with foil. Cook for 40–45 minutes until really tender, then leave to cool in the liquid before serving.

Home-preserved lemons

- Makes 8
  1 × 1l (375¾ fl oz) Kilner (Mason) jar
- Takes 30 minutes plus overnight resting

Preserved lemons are an invaluable addition to any pantry, offering a straightforward way to lift and transform dishes with their bright, tangy flavour. Easy to prepare and capable of lasting up to three months in your fridge, these lemons embody the art of preservation.

I often incorporate preserved lemons into salads to enhance the freshness of the ingredients. They are also fantastic in stews, where they add something of a warm depth and distinctive zestiness that enriches the overall flavours. Once you have a jar of preserved lemons to hand, you'll soon discover countless ways to infuse your meals with their vibrant flavour.

12 lemons
8 tbsp flaky sea salt
2 tbsp caster (superfine) sugar
1 tbsp coriander seeds
good pinch of chilli flakes
2 bay leaves

Wash the lemons and sterilise your jar (page 32). Cut the top and bottom off 8 of the lemons, then stand them on one end and cut almost into quarters, leaving them attached at the bottom.

Mix the salt and sugar together, then open out each lemon slightly and fill with the salt mixture.

Pack the lemons into the jar snugly, pushing down to fit them in, then seal and leave overnight.

The next day, juice the remaining 4 lemons and pour over the lemons to cover. Add the coriander seeds, chilli flakes and bay leaves. Seal and leave for at least a month before using.

The Spanish Pantry

Chocolate-coated candied lemon

- Makes 30 pieces
- Takes 1 hour cooling plus overnight drying

Tucked away in Barbate is a small family-run bakery called Tres Martínez, a place that truly stands out for me as one of the finest. Here, they stick to tradition with a real commitment to exceptional quality and flavour. Stepping into their shop is always such a delight; unlike many modern bakeries, Tres Martínez uses fresh eggs rather than the powdered mixes so common elsewhere, even in the most reputable places. I love seeing the piles of eggs ready to be used. I have even hoped to send someone there to learn from them, a dream I hope to see fulfilled one day. Among their many delights is their candied lemon, orange and ginger, which are particularly irresistible.

Inspired by their artisanal approach, here's my recipe for candied citrus peels dipped in dark chocolate. It's a special treat that marries the zesty brightness of citrus with the deep richness of dark chocolate.

4 unwaxed lemons
300g (10½oz /1⅔ cups) caster (superfine) sugar
2 tbsp glucose syrup
300ml (10fl oz/1¼ cups) water
150g (5oz) dark chocolate (50—70% cocoa solids, depending on taste)

Score the lemons with a sharp knife into quarters and carefully peel. Keep the flesh for another recipe. With your knife, remove most of the white pith from the skins.

Slice the skins into strips about 1cm (½in) thick. Put the skins in a saucepan of cold water, bring to the boil and boil for 1 minute, then drain and repeat twice more.

In a pan, melt the sugar and syrup with the water and bubble until you have a light syrup. Add the lemon peel and cook on a very gentle simmer for about 1 hour until tender and translucent. Allow them to cool in the pan.

Remove the peel and set on a wire rack and allow to dry at room temperature for 24 hours.

Melt the chocolate in a heatproof bowl set over a pan of gently simmering water. Carefully dip one end of each of the peels into the chocolate and return to the wire rack to dry.

Tip

You can also dry the lemons in a very low oven if you don't want to wait 24 hours before coating.

Requesón

- Makes about 600ml (20fl oz/2½ cups)
- Takes 1½ hours plus standing and chilling

Requesón is one of the most adaptable cheeses I know, fitting into both savoury and sweet contexts alike. Its mild, creamy texture makes it an excellent canvas for many flavours. In one of the recipes featured (page 140), I pair it with courgettes and preserved lemons, a combination that truly enhances its delicate taste.

For this particular preparation, I've chosen to enliven the milk by infusing it with a blend of aniseed, chillies, cloves and peppercorns. This mix introduces a dynamic spectrum of tastes – warm, spicy and subtly sweet – which combines beautifully with the preserved lemons, creating an overall balance that brings the dish to life.

If you're looking for a simple way to enjoy this cheese, try spreading it on toast with a touch of preserved lemon and a drizzle of good honey. This easy treat lets the requesón's versatility shine through.

To further experiment with the infusion process, start with bold flavours like star anise and chilli. These, especially when paired with the bright, complex notes of preserved lemons, provide a contrast that can transform requesón into something extraordinary.

1 litre (34fl oz/4 cups) whole unhomogenised milk
3 cloves
1 star anise
good pinch of chilli flakes
10 black peppercorns
good pinch of flaky sea salt
juice of 2–3 lemons

To make the curd cheese, heat the milk with the cloves, star anise, chilli flakes, peppercorns and salt until it reaches 85°C (185°F) on a digital thermometer. Remove from the heat and add the juice of 1 lemon and stir.

Leave to stand for 10 minutes until the curds have separated from the whey; you may need to add a little more lemon juice, a tablespoon at a time.

Line a colander with a muslin (cheesecloth) and stand it over a bowl. Pour the contents of the pan through the muslin. Remove the whole spices, if you can, and leave to stand for 30 minutes.

Gently squeeze any liquid from the curds. Once cool, tip the curds into a container and chill until ready to serve. It will keep in the fridge for 3–4 days.

Citrus-baked salmon

- Serves 4
- Takes 40 minutes

Citrus and salmon are a match made in heaven – the juicy lemon and sweet oranges brilliantly cut through the richness of the fish, unifying all the flavours in a pleasing harmony. In this recipe, roasting the citrus alongside the salmon not only infuses the fish with a warm, caramelised citrus flavour but it also enhances the overall feel of the dish. The addition of finely sliced fennel and a hint of red chilli brings a bit of texture and a touch of heat, making this combination not just vibrant but also really flavourful.

Whether served hot, straight from the oven, or cold in a refreshing salad, this simple, elegant dish is always satisfying. It's the kind of meal that brightens up the table with its bold colours and flavours. I'd recommend a nice rosé cava with this dish.

2 oranges or blush oranges
1 lemon
1 fennel bulb, finely sliced, fronds
    reserved
1 red chilli, finely sliced
3 tbsp olive oil
800g (1lb 12oz) piece of salmon
½ tsp sweet smoked pimentón
flaky sea salt and freshly ground
    black pepper

Preheat the oven to 170°C fan (180°C/350°F/gas 4). Slice the oranges and lemon into rounds and toss in a roasting tin with the fennel and chilli and half the oil. Season well with salt and pepper. Roast for 15 minutes.

Season the salmon with salt, pepper and the pimentón and place on top of the citrus and fennel, then return to the oven and roast for a further 15–20 minutes until the salmon is just cooked. Serve scattered with fennel fronds.

Sweet citrus jelly

- Makes 4–5 × 370g (13oz) jars
- Takes 2 hours plus overnight standing

This preserve is a jar of sunshine, ensuring your pantry contains the vibrant essence of the Mediterranean. It's versatile and enhances everything from cheese boards to dressings and desserts with its bright, zesty flair. Striking the perfect balance between sweetness and tang, it captures the quintessential flavours of the Mediterranean coast, adding a twist to everything it meets. Whether drizzled over Manchego fritters or swirled into a dessert, the preserve not only complements the flavours with which it is paired but takes them up a notch too. It's a must-have for any cooking enthusiast who wants to bring a touch of life to the table.

4 blood oranges
6 clementines
3 unwaxed lemons
1.5 litres (56fl oz/6⅔ cups) cold water
about 800g (1lb 12oz/4 cups) jam sugar

Cut each citrus fruit in 8 pieces, and tip into a large saucepan and cover with the cold water. Bring to the boil, then simmer gently for about 1 hour until the liquid has reduced by about half and the fruit is really soft.

Line a colander with a very large square of muslin (cheesecloth) and place over a large bowl. Tip the fruit and liquid into the lined colander, then tie the muslin square around the pulp and hang it so it drips into the bowl below. Leave overnight.

In the morning, discard the pulp and measure the juice. Do not squeeze the bag or the jelly will be cloudy. Pour into a large preserving pan and add the same weight of sugar in grams (ounces or cups) as you have millilitres (fluid ounces or cups) of juice.

Sterilise the jam jars and lids (page 32). Put a couple of little plates in the freezer for testing the set of your jelly.

Put the pan over a low heat and cook until the sugar has all dissolved, then increase the heat and boil and bubble vigorously until you reach setting point (104°C (220°F)). To test for a set, remove from the heat and pour a little onto one of your cold plates. It should wrinkle when you push it with your finger. If it doesn't quite feel set enough, return the pan to the heat and boil for another 1–2 minutes, then test again.

Once you have reached setting point, carefully ladle into the sterilised jars and top each one with a wax disc. Allow to cool, then seal, label and store in a cool dark place for up to a year.

Simple orange ice cream

- Serves 6 (in shells) with extra ice cream left over
- Takes 1½ hours plus chilling

The vivid memory of heading to the local shop to indulge in that scoop of orange ice cream remains clearly etched in my mind. This recipe transports me back to those carefree childhood days in Talaván, though the flavour here is markedly different – pure and unadulterated, free from any additives. Despite the cleaner taste of this homemade version, the orange ice cream from my childhood will always be a favourite, even though I know I'm probably embellishing the quality of it in my memory! There's just a charm about it that holds a special place in my heart, a sweet reminder of simpler times.

7 large oranges, chilled in the fridge overnight
750ml (26fl oz/generous 3 cups) double (heavy) cream, well chilled
200g (7oz/heaped 1 cup) caster (superfine) sugar
1 tsp vanilla bean paste
grating of orange zest, to serve

Take one of the oranges and finely grate the zest and squeeze out the juice. Discard the skin.

Cut the tops off the remaining oranges and use a sharp knife or grapefruit spoon to cut out the pulp from the middle, scraping the last pieces out with a spoon. Put the empty shells in the freezer.

Blend the pulp in a blender, then push through a sieve into a jug and add the zest and juice you have from the single orange.

Tip the juice back into the blender and add the cream, sugar and vanilla bean paste. Blend well, then pour into an ice cream maker and churn until set.

Scoop the ice cream into the frozen shells, return to the freezer and freeze overnight. Serve with a grating of orange zest.

Tip

This makes more than you need to fill the oranges so keep the rest in a tub for another time.

The Spanish Pantry

Orange-roast peaches
with honey and lavender

- Serves 6
- Takes 30 minutes

The arrival of stone-fruit season always brings me so much joy – it's a time of anticipation and celebration. Although it takes a couple of weeks for the very best of the season to reach its peak, the wait is well worth it. This recipe has quickly become a firm favourite at Iris, our home in Andalusia, loved by both our friends and guests. We often pair it with my partner Peter's almond cake (page 108) and a carefully curated cheese board featuring some of the finest cheeses from the region, making it the perfect centrepiece for a shared table.

When it comes to honey, I'm particularly fond of the exceptional varieties from Prado del Rey in Cádiz and Las Hurdes in Extremadura. Their deep, rich, sophisticated flavours are unparalleled and since they're not overly sweet, as honey should be, they complement the natural sweetness of stone fruits beautifully, adding an extra layer of indulgence to this simple yet stunning dish.

6 ripe yellow peaches
2 oranges
3 tbsp honey
2 sprigs of lavender, leaves picked
vanilla ice cream, to serve

Preheat the oven to 160°C fan (180°C/350°F/gas 4).

Cut a cross on the bottom of the peaches, then plunge them into a pan of boiling water for 20 seconds, then scoop out with a slotted spoon into a bowl of iced water.

Peel the peaches and put them in a small roasting tin. Zest one of the oranges and juice both. Blend the juice and zest with the honey, then pour over the peaches. Scatter with the lavender.

Roast for 20–25 minutes until sticky and tender. Serve with vanilla ice cream.

The Spanish Pantry

Citrus salsa with salt-baked tuna belly

- Serves 4
- Takes 40 minutes

When my friend Brendan proposed the idea of organising a *ronqueo* in London – a fascinating event where a whole tuna is expertly and skilfully butchered before your eyes – I was immediately captivated by the challenge. Naturally, I embraced the opportunity with enthusiasm and, as expected, it was an experience to remember.

The highlight of the event was undoubtedly the tuna belly, which we prepared by baking it in a thick crust of sea salt. This technique not only sealed in the flavours but also perfectly accentuated the tender, rich texture of the fish. To complement the fatty richness of the tuna belly, we served it alongside a vibrant citrus salsa. This added a burst of refreshing acidity that perfectly balanced the tuna's natural oils, taking it up a notch and creating a memorable experience. I'm so thankful to my friend from Gadira for making this happen.

750g (12lb 10oz) coarse sea salt
2 sprigs of thyme, leaves stripped
500g (1lb 2oz) piece of fatty tuna

For the salsa
2 lemons
3 oranges
1 red onion, finely sliced
a few sprigs of marjoram,
    leaves stripped
5 tbsp extra virgin olive oil
flaky sea salt

Preheat the oven to 180°C fan (200°C/400°F/gas 6).

Mix the salt and thyme with enough water to make it feel like wet sand. Spread a layer of the salt on a baking tray and put the tuna on top, then cover the tuna completely with the rest of the salt.

Bake in the oven for 15–20 minutes.

Meanwhile, make the salsa. Pare the skin off the lemons and oranges, then slice out the segments and roughly chop. Squeeze any juice from the membranes into the bowl. Add the red onion, plenty of sea salt, the marjoram and oil and leave to macerate.

Once the tuna has baked, remove from the oven and crack off the salt. Slice the fish and serve with the salsa.

Confit lemon with courgettes and requesón

- Serves 4
- Takes 20 minutes

This salad celebrates vibrant, fresh flavours, encapsulating the sunny essence of Mediterranean food. The tangy preserved lemons introduce a decent burst of citrus that harmonises with the creamy, subtly spiced requesón. Crisp courgettes contribute a refreshing texture, rounding out the dish with their lightness. This is simple to prepare yet wonderfully complex in flavour. The salad captures the happiness in Spanish cooking, making it an ideal, bright accompaniment to balance the richness of anything like hearty stews or just as a light lunch on a hot day.

3 courgettes (zucchini)
2 pieces preserved lemons (page 126)
good pinch of chilli flakes, plus extra
    to garnish
1 tsp coriander seeds, crushed
good squeeze of lemon juice
3 tbsp extra virgin olive oil, plus extra
    to drizzle
handful of small mint leaves, chopped
handful of fennel fronds or dill,
    roughly chopped
120g (4oz) requesón (page 130),
    crumbled
flaky sea salt and freshly ground
    black pepper

Slice the courgettes very thinly on the diagonal and tip into a large bowl.

Remove and discard the flesh from the preserved lemons and finely slice the skin. Add the skin to the courgettes in the bowl along with the chilli flakes, coriander seeds, lemon juice and oil as well as half the mint and fennel fronds. Season really well with salt and pepper, then toss together and spoon onto a serving dish. Scatter with the requesón cheese and the rest of the herbs, a sprinkle of the chilli flakes and a drizzle of olive oil and serve.

Duck and citrus salad

- Serves 4–6
- Takes 3 hours

The pairing of citrus with rich meats such as duck has an established history, rooted in centuries of traditional cooking techniques. Brought to Europe through ancient trade routes, citrus fruits were highly valued for their vibrant, sharp flavours that elegantly complemented the dense richness of robust meats. In the more sun-drenched regions of the Mediterranean, where oranges and lemons flourish, this combination became particularly valued, loved for the way it would bring together bold, fatty depth with fresh, citric flavours.

This recipe offers a contemporary twist: the duck needs to be roasted to perfection, its skin crisp, and sticky from the luscious orange glaze and having a gorgeous tanginess.

Accompanying the duck here is a fresh citrus salad, bursting with zestiness and providing a crunchy contrast that elevates the duck. This version of a timeless culinary duo proves that some combinations are indeed timeless, continuing to delight and inspire us even after centuries. This makes a special weekend dinner or a winner for festive occasions. A pale rosé, dry and crisp, would be my drink of choice for this dish.

1 large free-range duck
2 bay leaves
zest and juice of 2 oranges
30g (1oz/2 tbsp) light soft brown
    sugar
2 tbsp Pedro Ximénez sherry vinegar
½ tsp sweet smoked pimentón
1 tsp coriander seeds
120g (4oz) slightly stale bread, torn
flaky sea salt and freshly ground
    black pepper

For the salad
2 oranges
2 grapefruit
1 lemon
100g (3½oz) watercress
2 red chicory (Belgian endive)
1 tbsp honey
5 tbsp extra virgin olive oil

Bring the duck out of the fridge and set on a wire rack over a roasting tin. Prick all over with a skewer and allow to come to room temperature for 1 hour, then put the bay leaves inside and rub the skin with plenty of salt.

Preheat the oven to 180°C fan (200°C/400°F/gas 6).

Roast the duck for 45 minutes, then flip over, pouring off and reserving the fat. Return the duck to roast breast-side down for 45 minutes.

Segment the citrus fruits for the salad, reserving the juice.

In a saucepan, put the juice and zest from the 2 oranges with the sugar, sherry vinegar, pimentón, coriander seeds and some pepper and bubble gently until sticky.

Once the duck has roasted for 1½ hours, flip it back over and pour off any fat and also the juices from the roasting duck. Separate the fat and juice and add the juice to the pan with the orange glaze. Pour this all over the duck and return to the oven for 15 minutes, then allow to rest on its trivet over the tin.

Meanwhile, heat 3 tablespoons of the reserved fat in a pan and fry the bread until golden and crispy. Drain on paper towels and season with salt.

Arrange the watercress and chicory on a platter and scatter with the citrus segments.

To make the dressing, mix 3 tablespoons of the reserved juices with the honey and plenty of seasoning and, then whisk in the extra virgin olive oil. Pour over the salad.

Remove as much meat as you can from the duck and shred or slice, then toss in the sticky sauce that has collected in the roasting tin.

Scatter the sticky duck over the salad along with the crispy crumbs and serve.

Lecha frita with caramel oranges

- Serves 8
- Takes 1 hour plus chilling

This has always been a favourite dessert in our family, and my mum, Isabel has mastered it beautifully. If you translate *leche frita* literally, it comes out as 'fried milk' which, of course, doesn't make much sense! It's actually a creamy custard made from milk, flour, cornflour and sugar. The custard is then chilled until firm, cut into squares, coated in flour and egg, and fried until golden.

For the caramel oranges
5 oranges
100g (3½oz/heaped ½ cup) caster (superfine) sugar
2 tbsp water

For the leche
750ml (26fl oz/generous 3 cups) whole milk
1 cinnamon stick
1 vanilla pod, split and seeds scraped out
100g (3½oz/heaped ½ cup) caster (superfine) sugar, plus 2 tbsp to dust
50g (2oz/heaped ⅓ cup) plain (all-purpose) flour, plus 2 tbsp, to dust
30g (1oz/2 tbsp) cornflour (cornstarch)
2 medium free-range egg yolks
150ml (5fl oz/scant ⅔ cup) olive oil, plus extra for greasing
2 free-range eggs, beaten
½ tsp ground cinnamon

To prepare the oranges, pare all the skin from 4 of the oranges, then slice the fruit and put into a bowl. Juice the last orange and tip into a jug (you should have about 100ml (3½fl oz/scant ½ cup)). Use a sharp knife to remove all the pith from one of the orange skins. Grease a medium baking tray with olive oil and set aside.

To make the leche, put the pared orange zest in a saucepan with the milk, cinnamon and vanilla and heat gently until almost boiling. Remove from the heat and leave to stand for 20 minutes to infuse.

Meanwhile, continue with the oranges. Put the sugar and water in a pan and melt gently over a low heat, then increase the heat and bubble until you have a dark golden caramel. Remove the pan from the heat (as it will sputter and spit) and pour in the orange juice, then pour over the oranges and set aside to cool, then chill until needed.

To continue with the leche, blend the sugar, the 2 tablespoons of the flour and the cornflour in a bowl and strain over 100ml (3½fl oz/scant ½ cup) of the milk. Whisk to combine to a smooth paste before adding the rest of the milk and the egg yolks. Add the mixture to the pan over a medium heat for 10–15 minutes, whisking, until it becomes thick.

Pour into the baking tray (so it is about 2.5cm (1in) thick), cover with clingfilm (plastic wrap) and chill for at least 3 hours, or better overnight.

Carefully turn out the chilled leche and slice into 2cm (¾in) squares. Heat the oil in a wok or pan. Dip the leche squares in beaten egg, then in the 2 tablespoons of flour and fry for about 1 minute on each side until golden. Drain on paper towels, then dust with the 2 tablespoons of sugar and cinnamon and serve with the oranges.

The Spanish Pantry

Citrus and lemon thyme Spanish gin and tonic

- Serves 2
- Takes 15 minutes plus chilling

The British may have invented the gin and tonic, but the Spanish truly mastered it. Its history goes back to the 18th century, when British officers in India mixed gin with tonic water to make quinine – a remedy for malaria – more palatable. Citrus, added to balance the bitterness, quickly became an essential part of the drink.

Gin and tonic began to gain popularity in Spain in the late 20th century, and by the 1990s, Spanish bartenders had transformed it into an art form. You may have noticed that in traditional and local bars in Spain, there's no measuring – they just pour the gin until it feels right or until you say stop. Served in large balloon glasses with plenty of ice, the Spanish appreciate the balance of flavours and refreshing simplicity.

While some places load their glasses with an array of herbs and fruits, I prefer to keep things simple. I'm not a fan of turning a gin and tonic into a botanical garden. This one is my perfect gin and tonic – simple, refreshing and very Spanish.

2 lemons
1 lime
60g (2oz/⅓ cup) caster (superfine) sugar
4 sprigs of lemon thyme
100ml (3½fl oz/scant ½ cup) gin
tonic water, to top up

Squeeze the lemons and lime and put the juice into a saucepan with the sugar and lemon thyme. Heat gently to melt the sugar, then boil until lightly syrupy. Pour into a small jug and chill.

Put 2 large wine glasses in the freezer to chill.

Fill the glasses with ice, then add a double measure of gin to each. Divide the syrup between the glasses, then top up with tonic and serve.

Rice

Many people outside Spain don't always realise that rice is a favourite and significant part of Spanish cooking. However, it wasn't always such an everyday ingredient. Brought to Spain by the Moors in the 8th century, it found the perfect home in the marshlands of Valencia, Murcia and parts of Extremadura, where the climate made it easy to grow. At first, rice was considered to be a bit of a luxury, often saved for special occasions and even being used as an instrument of trade, functioning as hard currency. Over time, it became part of regular family meals and food traditions across Spain.

As the use of rice spread, each region developed its own prized recipes by mixing it with local ingredients. One of my all-time favourite dishes is Arroz al horno with pork ribs (page 158), where the slow-cooked meat releases its rich flavour into the grains, creating a hearty and comforting meal. It's one of the popular dishes at my pub, The Swan Inn, Claygate. Another favourite is Squid stuffed with ink and morcilla rice (page 154) where the soft, mild squid balances with the deep, savoury taste of the sausage, blending stunning flavours from both land and sea – something we call *mar y montaña* in Spain.

Then, of course, there's paella, arguably the most famous Spanish rice dish known throughout the world. Originally from Valencia, paella combines short-grain rice, saffron, meats, seafood and seasonal vegetables, all cooked together to let the rice soak up all the flavour. It has become an iconic symbol of Spanish cuisine, celebrated for its vibrant colours, rich flavours and deep-rooted traditions. From a rare ingredient to a regular favourite, various types of rice and different recipes have become central to Spanish cooking. Each region has its own special rice recipes that the people hold dear, adding to Spain's rich food traditions and bringing flavours of our diverse country to the table. Rice is incredibly adaptable and it soaks up flavours easily, making it perfect for everything from simple family dinners to big celebrations. Whether cooked with meats, seafood or fresh vegetables, rice brings everything together, creating dishes that feel both homely and remarkably special.

Sobrasada rice with crispy artichokes

- Serves 4
- Takes 1 hour

Sobrasada is something truly special, particularly the way it melts when cooked. It turns into a silky, luxurious texture, releasing its rich, spiced oils that add an intense, meaty depth of flavour. This is what makes it so unique in Spanish cooking – it creates a warmth and complexity.

This recipe is not just a personal favourite, but is also top seller across our José Pizarro restaurants. The flavourful creamy rice topped with crispy artichokes is the perfect combination of sophistication and fun. When you cook the rice with stock infused by the sobrasada, you achieve something incredible: deeply rich, spicy, slightly smoky, with a touch of sweetness.

If you're short on time, use preserved artichokes instead of crispy ones. Just drain them, pat dry and serve on top of the rice.

4 small/medium fresh globe
   artichokes
squeeze of lemon juice
3 tbsp olive oil, plus 750ml (26fl oz/
   generous 3 cups), for deep-frying
2 banana shallots, finely chopped
150g (5oz) sobrasada
300g (10½oz/scant 1⅔ cups) bomba
   or other medium-grain paella rice
100ml (3½fl oz/scant ½ cup)
   dry white wine
800ml (28fl oz/3½ cups) fresh
   chicken stock
flaky sea salt and freshly ground
   black pepper

Tip

You could also use the Olive oil-braised artichokes with lemon (page 124) instead of making crispy ones and serve them on top of the rice at the end.

Prepare the artichokes. Trim the stems, then remove the tough outer leaves, pulling them away from the main globe. Do this until you see a colour change to a lighter pale green. Cut off the top one-third of the artichoke to remove the spines, then cut in half lengthways. Scoop out any of the feathery choke, then put into water with a good squeeze of lemon juice.

Put a steamer basket over boiling water and steam the artichokes for 20 minutes until tender to the tip of a knife. Allow to cool, then cut each half in half again (so you end up with 16 quarters).

Meanwhile, heat the 3 tablespoons of oil in a sauté pan and gently fry the shallots for 5 minutes until tender. Add the sobrasada, break up with a spoon and fry, increasing the heat a little, until it has all broken down and smells delicious. Add the rice and toss with the oily juices.

Add the wine and bubble for a minute, then pour in all the stock and season well. Reduce to a simmer and cook for 15–20 minutes until the rice is tender but still quite soupy.

As the rice is cooking, heat the the remaining oil in a deep pan to 170°C (340°F) and fry the artichokes for 2–3 minutes until really golden and crispy. Drain on paper towels and season with salt.

Spoon the rice into bowls and top with the crispy artichokes.

Squid stuffed with ink and morcilla rice

- Serves 4
- Takes 50 minutes

Morcilla de Burgos is one of Spain's favourites, and it has rightfully earned acclaim both domestically and internationally. Originating from Burgos in northern Spain, this iconic sausage is distinguished by its unique incorporation of rice, a practice dating back to the 18th century, which absorbs the rich juices during cooking and gives the morcilla its characteristic texture.

The sausage is packed full of flavours, with the earthy notes of onion and garlic, enriched with lard and seasoned with a bold blend of spices including paprika, black pepper and nutmeg. The hint of parsley or oregano adds a fresh dimension, making it more complex still.

Paired with sweet, tender squid, morcilla de Burgos just delights our taste buds. Grilling the squid introduces a caramelised exterior that goes beautifully with the deep, savoury notes of the sausage, creating a clever contrast that is nothing short of divine.

To truly celebrate this dish, enjoy it with a glass of robust Ribera del Duero red wine, enhancing the flavours. This pairing is not just a meal, but a food lover's heaven.

2 tbsp olive oil
300g (10½oz) morcilla, sliced
1 small onion, finely chopped
150g (5oz/heaped ¾ cup) bomba or other medium-grain paella rice
100ml (3½fl oz/scant ½ cup) white wine or fino sherry
1 sachet squid or cuttlefish ink
8 small squid, cleaned
extra virgin olive oil, for drizzling
flaky sea salt and freshly ground black pepper
lemon wedges, to serve

Heat the oil in a sauté pan and fry the morcilla over a medium heat until golden brown, then remove to a plate and set aside.

Add the onion to the pan and fry gently for 5 minutes until softened, then add the rice and toss to coat in the hot oil. Add the wine and cook for 1–2 minutes then add the ink. Season to taste then allow to cool a little.

Stuff the squid with the rice, then season the squid with salt and pepper. Heat a heavy-based pan or plancha over a high heat and quickly sear the stuffed squid.

Serve on a bed of any of rice and with a drizzle of extra virgin olive oil and a wedge of lemon.

The Spanish Pantry

Rabbit rice with rosemary and oregano

- Serves 4–6
- Takes 1 hour plus overnight marinating

Rabbit is a fantastic meat that I believe we should enjoy more often. It's plentiful, low in fat, and offers excellent value for money. Marinating the rabbit overnight really brings out the flavours and makes the meat tender. In Spain, you'll find rabbits in fields surrounded by wild herbs like oregano and rosemary, so the ideal additions to your marinade are suggested by nature herself. If you change your mind the next day after marinating and decide to grill it instead, garnish it with the warm gigante beans on toast from page 195 and you'll have a very happy day.

My preferred pairing would be a glass of oloroso or palo cortado with this dish, served in a wine glass, of course – there isn't anything more sumptuous.

1 rabbit, portioned
4 tbsp olive oil
4 sprigs of oregano
2 sprigs of rosemary
2 tbsp cider vinegar
2 banana shallots, finely chopped
125ml (4fl oz/½ cup) fino sherry
500ml (17fl oz/2 cups) fresh dark chicken stock
1 tbsp tomato purée (paste)
350g (12oz/scant 2 cups) bomba or other medium-grain paella rice
flaky sea salt and freshly ground black pepper
crusty bread, to serve

Marinate the rabbit in 2 tablespoons of the oil with the herbs and vinegar overnight.

The next day, heat a large, flat casserole or paella pan and brown the rabbit all over. Remove to a plate.

Heat the remaining oil and gently fry the shallots for 5 minutes, then return the rabbit to the pan, add the sherry and bubble for 1 minute. Pour over three-quarters of the chicken stock and stir in the tomato purée. Season with salt and pepper and simmer gently for 40 minutes until the rabbit is tender and the sauce is thick and reduced.

Add the rice and the rest of the stock and simmer for 12–15 more minutes until the rice is tender and the sauce slightly soupy. Serve with crusty bread.

Arroz al horno with pork ribs

- Serves 6
- Takes 3 hours plus marinating

Ribs have a special place in my heart – they're just irresistible, no matter how they're cooked! In this recipe, while rice serves as the foundational ingredient, the ribs are the star of the show. Marinated to perfection, the ribs release their rich, savoury juices into the rice as they cook, infusing every grain with a depth of flavour that is mouth-watering and satisfying.

The marinade is a bold mix of aromatics and spices, including the zest of lemon and sprigs of fresh oregano, enhanced by a good pinch of pimentón. Marinating not only tenderises the ribs but deepens the flavours. As the ribs slow-cook to tender perfection, their flavours combine with the lemon's acidity, cutting through the richness and balancing the fatty succulence of the pork.

This harmonious blend of tender meat, aromatic seasoning and refreshing citrus results in a dish in which the flavours dance together in unison. Paired with the soft, flavourful rice that captures all the essences of the marinade, this dish is both hearty and refined.

An Amontillado would pair beautifully with these delicious ribs.

6 chunky pork belly ribs
200ml (7fl oz/scant 1 cup) white wine
pared zest of 1 lemon
4 sprigs of oregano
good pinch of pimentón
75ml (2½fl oz/scant ⅓ cup) olive oil
1 large onion, finely sliced
2 red (bell) peppers, deseeded and sliced
3 large tomatoes, chopped
3 garlic cloves, crushed
300g (10½oz/1⅔ cups) bomba or other medium-grain paella rice
700ml (24fl oz/3 cups) fresh chicken stock
flaky sea salt and freshly ground black pepper

Put the ribs in a dish with the white wine, lemon zest, oregano and pimentón and marinate for 1–2 hours, or overnight.

Preheat the oven to 140°C fan (160°C/320°F/gas 2–3). Put the ribs in an ovenproof dish and cover with kitchen foil. Bake for 2 hours, or until tender.

Meanwhile, heat the oil in a paella pan or ovenproof dish. Fry the onion and peppers for 10 minutes until really softened, then add the tomatoes and garlic and cook for 5 more minutes.

Increase the oven temperature to 170°C fan (190°C/375°F/gas 5).

Add the rice to the pan, then nestle the ribs into the rice, pouring in any of their juices. Pour over the stock, season well with salt and pepper and return to the oven. Bake for 40–45 minutes until the rice is tender and the ribs are browned, then serve.

Salted arroz con leche

- Serves 4
- Takes 1 hour

This isn't the kind of rice pudding you'd normally find in a Spanish home, but it's absolutely beautiful. Inspired by my travels in India, it's flavoured with warm spices like cardamom and cinnamon, which give it a rich and aromatic twist. The little pinch of salt might sound surprising, but it works magic, balancing the sweetness perfectly. Creamy, fragrant and so full of flavour, this is a dessert that takes me back to vibrant Rajasthan. Simple ingredients, unforgettable flavours – this pudding is something truly special.

250g (9oz/heaped 1⅓ cups) bomba or other medium-grain paella rice
pared zest of 1 lemon
3 cardamom pods, cracked
1 cinnamon stick
1 litre (34fl oz/4 cups) whole milk
100g (3½oz/heaped ¾ cup) caster (superfine) sugar
1 tsp flaky sea salt
200ml (7fl oz/scant 1 cup) double (heavy) cream
light soft brown sugar, to taste, for sprinkling

Put the rice, lemon zest, spices and milk in a saucepan and add the sugar and salt. Bring to a simmer and cook gently for 45 minutes–to 1 hour until the rice is very tender and much of the milk has absorbed but it's still creamy.

Remove from the heat and add the cream. Serve with a little soft brown sugar for sprinkling.

Wild rice salad with home-smoked mackerel

- Serves 4
- Takes 1 hour

Wild rice might not be something you'd typically find in Spanish cooking – our kitchens usually lean towards short-grain rice like bomba for dishes like paella. But at home, I love experimenting with it, even though it doesn't make it onto my restaurant menus.

Smoking fish at home is easier than you might think, and the flavour you get is incredible.

If you're short on time or don't want to smoke your own fish, good-quality, market-smoked mackerel or hot smoked salmon works just as well. It's also fantastic with barbecued chicken or even on its own as a filling, healthy meal.

For the smoked mackerel
1 tbsp flaky sea salt
8 mackerel fillets
200g (7oz/heaped 1 cup) white long-grain rice
1 tbsp caster (superfine) sugar
tiny handful of beech or other wood chips

For the rice
125g (4oz/¾ cup) wild rice
1 lemon, segmented
1 small red onion, finely sliced
½ cucumber, deseeded and diced
handful of flat-leaf parsley, chopped
4 tbsp extra virgin olive oil
flaky sea salt and freshly ground black pepper

Rub the salt all over the fish and set aside.

Take a large stainless steel wok (not non-stick) and make sure a round wire rack sits inside. Line the wok with 1 or 2 large pieces of kitchen foil so it comes up past the side, then add the white rice, sugar and beech chips and cover with the rack.

Place the fish on the wire rack, then cover with a domed lid, so the foil is on the outside. Make sure the windows are open and the extractor fan is switched on.

Place over a low heat and as soon as you see wisps of smoke, use the foil to seal the wok and lid, using an extra strip of foil to make sure it is secure. Cook over a low heat for about 15 minutes. Turn off the heat and leave to stand for at least 10 minutes before uncovering and removing the fish.

Put the wild rice in a pan of cold salted water, bring to the boil, then cook for 40 minutes until tender and starting to split. Drain well and allow to steam under a tea towel.

Chop the lemon segments and toss with the onion, cucumber and parsley. Mix in the extra virgin olive oil and season to taste with salt and pepper.

Flake the mackerel and toss with the rice and salsa and serve.

Chickpeas

I love chickpeas so much that I've dedicated a whole chapter to them. They're more than just an ingredient to me – they're a part of my life, my memories, my connection to Extremadura and to Spain. I will always remember as a child watching the hardworking people of Talaván meticulously cleaning and sorting the dried pods after the harvest. They would separate the peas from the pods and sift, letting the breeze take the chaff. Only the finest chickpeas made the cut – those little golden treasures that had been grown and cleaned with such care. Watching them work, with their experienced hands and laughter filling the air, felt like being part of something bigger, something timeless.

Chickpeas were everywhere when I was growing up. They were the base of so many meals, from salads to stews. They were nothing fancy, but they were always satisfying, and always handled with care. Of course, nothing ever went to waste. Every single bean would be used, prepared in such ways to feed us when the months turned colder and the days became shorter. Extremadura, although hot in the summer, gets extremely cold in the winter; life was tough in rural Spain.

Rural people had to be creative and inventive to survive the challenges of extreme seasonal changes. The dish that best represents the hard work and resourcefulness of village life is the *cocido*, or stew. For us, it's way more than just a recipe; it's the story of how people made the most of what they had. My mum told me it was practically daily food for so many families, who stretched ingredients to feed everyone in the most creative way out of necessity. Over time, though, the stew has evolved into a real delicacy and each family has their own style. I love *cocido*. In fact, I loved it so much that my mum would even cook it for me in the summer when it was 40°C (104°F) outside – and she still does, no matter how hot it is outdoors. So now, whenever I cook with chickpeas, whether in *cocido* or any other dish, I think of those breezy days and the precious memories they hold. They remind me how something small can carry so much meaning – hard work, effort, nourishment but, more importantly, connection and enjoyment.

Moorish spiced crispy chickpeas

- Serves 6–8
- Takes 1 hour

Sometimes the perfect drink inspires the perfect snack. That's certainly the case with these Moorish spiced crispy chickpeas, which were born from a pairing with a chilled glass of Estrella Damm lager. The bold, aromatic spices of cumin, coriander and a hint of chilli powder make these chickpeas irresistibly tasty and a perfect companion to a cold beer on a warm summer afternoon or a relaxing evening indoors.

These little crispy delights are not only delicious but also practical, which I like. They can be stored in an airtight container for up to a month, making them an excellent snack to prepare in advance. However, their addictive flavour makes them hard to save so you'll probably find yourself reaching for 'just a few more'!

2 × 400g (14oz) tins of chickpeas (garbanzos), drained and rinsed
3 tbsp olive oil
1 tsp ground cumin
½ tsp ground coriander
good pinch of chilli powder
1 tsp flaky sea salt

Preheat the oven to 180°C fan (200°C/400°F/gas 6).

Mix the chickpeas with the olive oil, cumin, coriander, chilli powder and salt and spread over a large baking sheet. Roast in the oven, shaking occasionally, for 40–50 minutes until deeply golden and crisp.

Allow to cool before serving or storing in an airtight container.

Spinach, chickpea and dill albondigas

- Serves 6
- Takes 1 hour plus chilling

It surprises me when people phone my restaurants asking if we have vegetarian or vegan dishes, thinking we primarily serve dishes centred around pork and Manchego! Spanish cuisine is amazingly diverse, and we take great pride in offering a broad range of options that cater to everyone's tastes, including a fantastic selection of vegetarian and vegan dishes.

One standout example from our menu is the spinach, chickpea and dill *albóndigas* (meatballs). These are not only delicious but also visually appealing, making them a hit among our guests. This recipe can easily be adapted to a more substantial vegan meal by substituting the yoghurt with the Luxurious tomato sauce (page 34) and serving with crusty bread.

720g (1lb 9½oz) jar of chickpeas (garbanzos), drained and rinsed
200g (7oz) spinach
2 small courgettes (zucchini), coarsely grated
3 tbsp olive oil
75g (2½oz/¼ cup) fresh white breadcrumbs
2 garlic cloves, crushed
1 tsp smoked pimentón
25g (1oz) packed dill fronds, finely chopped
1 large egg
flaky sea salt and freshly ground black pepper

For the yoghurt dip
200g (7oz/scant 1 cup) Greek yoghurt
1 garlic clove, crushed
4 spring onions (scallions), finely sliced
2 tbsp extra virgin olive oil
good pinch of chilli flakes

Put the chickpeas in a food processor and whiz until well broken down.

Put the spinach in a large frying pan (skillet) over a medium-high heat with a splash of water and allow to wilt. Add the courgettes and cook together until all the moisture has evaporated. Season well with salt and pepper, then tip onto a plate to cool.

Return the pan to a medium heat, add 2 tablespoons of the olive oil, then the breadcrumbs, garlic and pimentón and fry together until lightly golden.

Use your hands to squeeze all the liquid you can out of the spinach and courgette, then add to the food processor. Add the golden crumbs, dill, egg and plenty of salt and pepper and blitz together to form a thick paste.

Roll the mixture into walnut-sized balls and chill in the fridge on a lined baking sheet for at least 1 hour.

Next, make the yoghurt dip by mixing the yoghurt with the garlic, spring onions and plenty of seasoning. Spoon into a dish, drizzle with the extra virgin olive oil and scatter with chilli flakes.

Heat the remaining olive oil in a large non-stick frying pan and fry the chickpea meatballs all over until golden and piping hot. Serve with the yoghurt dip.

The Spanish Pantry

Moorish goat and chickpea stew

- Serves 4–6
- Takes 4 hours

Goat meat isn't very popular in the UK, even though it's extremely healthy, low in fat and affordable. It's also straightforward to cook and tastes great in many recipes, from curries to roasts. If more people knew how simple it is to prepare, and how delicious it can be, goat meat would definitely become more common on UK menus and dinner tables.

My preference is to use baby goat, since the meat is tender and only needs about an hour to cook, making it perfect for a quick, flavourful meal. Ancho peppers work well as a swap for ñora peppers in this recipe, adding some smoky-sweet notes.

A Gran Reserva Rioja is a great choice with this dish, bringing out rich flavours and making the meal even more enjoyable.

3 tbsp olive oil
1kg (2lb 4oz) young goat meat, cubed
1 large onion, finely sliced
3 garlic cloves, crushed
2 tsp cumin seeds
3 dried choricero or ñora peppers
2 bay leaves
200ml (7fl oz/scant 1 cup) fino sherry
400ml (13fl oz/generous 1½ cups)
    dark chicken stock
400g (14oz) tin of chickpeas
    (garbanzos), drained and rinsed
handful of flat-leaf parsley, chopped
    (optional)
flaky sea salt and freshly ground
    black pepper
crusty bread, to serve

Heat the oil in a large casserole or heavy-based frying pan (skillet). Season the goat with plenty of salt and pepper and fry in the hot oil until browned all over. Set aside.

Add the onion to the pan and gently fry for 10 minutes, then add the garlic, cumin seeds, dried peppers and bay leaves and fry for a further 1–2 minutes.

Return the goat to the pan, add the sherry and bubble for 5–10 minutes until reduced by half. Add the chicken stock with plenty of seasoning, cover and simmer gently for 3 hours, or until the meat is very tender.

Add the chickpeas and continue to cook for a further 20 minutes with the lid off to help reduce the sauce further. Serve scattered with the parsley, if you like, and with a good quality crusty bread.

Tip

You can look out for ñora pepper paste and use 1–2 teaspoons instead of the dried peppers or you could use any smoky mild chilli pepper such as ancho.

Crispy fried red mullet with chickpea and red onion salad

- Serves 4
- Takes 30 minutes

Red mullet is one of the gems of the sea, one that I adore for its distinctive flavour, delicate texture and the charming 'smile' it seems to wear at the fish market – always a sight that brings me joy. This highly prized fish, particularly revered in the Andalusian coastal town of Barbate, is known for its range of sizes and for the versatility it offers in cooking methods. Whether it tips the scales at a few grams or approaches the heftier side of half a kilo, red mullet always delivers great taste and quality.

Best known for the way its sweet, nutty flavour – which some liken to a cross between crab and lobster – stands out whether it's grilled or pan-fried, red mullet is a winner. This recipe celebrates this delightful fish by pairing it with a wonderful chickpea salad, complementing the natural flavours with the freshness of the lemon and aromatic fennel seeds. The contrast between the warm fish and the cool herbaceous salad creates a food experience that is balanced and exciting.

4 tbsp chickpea (gram) flour
1 tsp smoked pimentón
8 red mullet fillets
75ml (2½fl oz/scant ⅓ cup) olive oil
flaky sea salt and freshly ground
    black pepper

For the salad
1 tbsp olive oil
1 garlic clove, bashed
1 tsp fennel seeds
2 × 400g (14oz) tins of chickpeas
    (garbanzos), drained and rinsed
1 red onion, finely chopped
juice of 1 lemon
3 tbsp extra virgin olive oil
large handful of flat-leaf parsley,
    leaves picked and chopped

Prepare the salad. Heat the oil, garlic and fennel seeds in a frying pan (skillet). Add the chickpeas and gently cook for 3–4 minutes, stirring, then tip into a large serving bowl and season well with salt and pepper.

Add the onion and lemon juice and set aside while you prepare the fish.

Mix the chickpea flour with the pimentón and plenty of salt and pepper. Dredge the red mullet fillets in the flour.

Heat the oil in a large frying pan (skillet) until it shimmers, then add the fillets and fry for 4–5 minutes until golden and crispy, turning once. Drain on paper towels.

Add the parsley to the salad and serve with the crispy red mullet fillets.

The Spanish Pantry

Chickpea flatbreads with mussels

- Serves 2–4
- Takes 30 minutes plus resting

This is my take on the classic socca, a traditional chickpea flatbread from the south of France. I prefer mine a little thinner for a lighter texture that absorbs the flavours of the toppings. Mussels and tinned tuna are the most popular combination, but I especially enjoy using mussels in escabeche. The tangy vinegar, aromatic spices and rich oils from the escabeche create a fantastic natural vinaigrette that perfectly complements the fresh, juicy toppings, soaking into the warm flatbread for an irresistible burst of flavour.

125g (4oz/1 cup) chickpea (gram) flour
good pinch of flaky sea salt
1 tsp cumin seeds
½ tsp smoked sweet pimentón
200–220ml (7–7½fl oz/scant 1 cup) water
3 tbsp olive oil, plus extra for drizzling
2 large ripe heirloom tomatoes, chopped
1 × 125g (4oz) tin of best-quality mussels in oil or in escabeche
3 spring onions (scallions), finely sliced

Put the chickpea flour into a bowl with the salt and spices. Add the water and olive oil and whisk until you have a thick batter. Leave to stand for at least 1 hour or up to 12 hours.

Heat a large cast-iron skillet over a high heat with a drizzle of oil, then pour in the batter. Cook for 3–4 minutes over a medium heat until the top is almost cooked and full of bubbles. Flip over and cook on the other side for 1–2 minutes.

Slide onto a board, then scatter with the tomatoes, mussels and spring onions. Drizzle with extra virgin olive oil and serve.

Oloroso-braised lamb shanks and chickpeas with warm anchovy salsa

- Serves 4
- Takes 4 hours

In Spain, we love lamb, particularly when it's very young and tender. Our favourite is, without a doubt, the suckling lamb, which is often slow-roasted to perfection and served as a whole leg or shoulder rather than in smaller cuts like the shank. Because of this tradition, lamb shanks aren't as commonly used in Spanish cooking as they are in other cuisines.

Interestingly, while chickpeas are a pantry essential in Spanish kitchens, you'll rarely find them paired with lamb in our recipes. Instead, chickpeas tend to be the star in dishes, while lamb is celebrated in simpler preparations that highlight its own, natural flavour. So this makes the combination of lamb and chickpeas an unusual but creative and intriguing opportunity to explore flavours beyond the traditional Spanish norms!

4 lamb shanks
4 tbsp olive oil
1 onion, finely chopped
1 celery stalk, finely chopped
1 carrot, finely chopped
3 garlic cloves, peeled
2 tbsp plain (all-purpose) flour
200ml (7fl oz/scant 1 cup) oloroso
    sherry
2 bay leaves
750ml (26fl oz/generous 3 cups)
    fresh chicken stock
700g (1½lb) jar chickpeas (garbanzo
    beans), drained
flaky sea salt and freshly ground
    black pepper

For the salsa
4 tbsp extra virgin olive oil
4 salted anchovy fillets, chopped
2 garlic cloves, finely sliced
2 large tomatoes, diced
large bunch flat-leaf parsley,
    finely chopped

Season the lamb shanks really well with salt and pepper. Heat half the olive oil in a flameproof casserole and brown the shanks all over. Remove to a plate and add the rest of the oil. Gently fry the onion, celery, carrot and garlic for 10 minutes until softened. Stir in the flour and cook for 1–2 minutes, then add the sherry and bubble for 2–3 minutes.

Add the bay leaves and stock, return the lamb to the pan and bring to the boil. Reduce to a simmer and cook gently, partially covered, for 3 hours until meltingly tender and the sauce has reduced. Add the chickpeas and stir until warmed through.

To make the salsa, heat the extra virgin olive oil in a pan over a low heat and gently warm the anchovies until they start to melt. Add the garlic and tomatoes and gently warm through with the anchovies for 1–2 minutes, then tip into a bowl and mix with the parsley and plenty of salt and pepper.

Serve the lamb shanks with the warm anchovy salsa.

The Spanish Pantry

Roast pumpkin and chickpeas with lemon and oregano

- Serves 4–6
- Takes 1 hour

This warm salad is perfect for a chilly autumn day, bringing together the earthy sweetness of roasted pumpkin with the hearty goodness of chickpeas. Flavoured with garlic, lemon, oregano and a hint of chilli, it's simple, comforting and full of flavour. Serve it as a main or a side, and enjoy it with a drizzle of olive oil and a squeeze of fresh lemon for a bright finish.

1 pumpkin, such as a Crown Prince (about 1.6kg (3lb 8oz))
3 tbsp olive oil
1 garlic bulb, cloves separated
good pinch of chilli flakes
finely grated zest of 1 lemon
6 sprigs of oregano, leaves stripped
400g (14oz) chickpeas (garbanzos), drained and rinsed
2 tbsp extra virgin olive oil
flaky sea salt and freshly ground black pepper
lemon wedges, to serve

Preheat the oven to 180°C fan (200°C/400°F/gas 6).

Cut the pumpkin into wedges and scoop out and discard the seeds. Arrange the wedges in a large roasting tin and toss with a little of the olive oil. Scatter in the garlic, chilli flakes and lemon zest and season well with salt and pepper.

Roast for 30 minutes, then turn the pieces and add the oregano and chickpeas and a drizzle more olive oil. Roast for a further 20 minutes. Drizzle with extra virgin olive oil and serve with lemon wedges.

Beans

Growing up, my mum always cooked beans until they were completely overcooked – so soft they turned into a purée, barely looking like beans any more. That's just how it was at home. For her, beans weren't done until they had melted into a thick, creamy base, soaking up all the garlic, olive oil and herbs. It was comforting and rich, something you could scoop up with bread, and to her, that was the only way beans should be cooked.

Now, when I make beans, I can't help but laugh at the reaction from my family. 'These are undercooked!' they always say, poking at them with their forks. I like them tender but still holding their shape. For me, it's about letting the beans shine while still soaking up all the wonderful flavours they're cooked with. But for my mum, it's unthinkable to serve beans that aren't practically a spread.

Beans were always part of our meals and they were tied to so many memories. My dad grew them in the garden every year, and I'd help him pick the pods, excited to see them on the table later in the day. Fresh or dried, they always went through the same slow cooking process – hours simmering on the stove, filling the house with the smell of olive oil and garlic.

Beans have been a staple of Spanish kitchens for centuries, with a history that stretches back to the arrival of legumes from the Americas in the 16th century. Over time, they became an essential part of our culinary traditions, appearing in dishes like *Fabada asturiana* (page 191), *potaje de vigilia*, and countless regional stews. Each region has its own special beans, from the small, creamy alubias of the north to the larger, earthier varieties grown in the south. They're simple, affordable and deeply versatile, making them a cornerstone of Spanish cooking.

In Spain, beans are more than just food – they're part of who we are. They're in the *potajes* and *fabadas*, the simple stews and slow-cooked dishes that bring everyone together around the table. My mum's beans were all about comfort, thick and hearty, perfect for mopping up with crusty bread. They remind me of home and of her way of cooking: simple, honest and full of love.

Clams with creamy white beans and bacon

- Serves 4
- Takes 40 minutes

White beans and clams or cockles are a beloved classic in northern Spain, particularly highly regarded in the culinary-rich regions of Galicia and Asturias – and, of course, at Pizarro restaurant, where the blending of land and sea creates beautiful flavours. This dish exemplifies everything I love about simplicity in Spanish cooking: creamy white beans absorb the briny, salty juices of fresh clams, resulting in a hearty, comforting meal that is bursting with the vibrant essence of coastal cuisine.

This dish shows how simple, humble ingredients can be easily enhanced through some traditional cooking methods, meticulous care and appreciation for honest, straightforward cooking. The flavours are both deep and delicate, making it a soul-soothing meal that feels both luxurious and familiar.

To fully enjoy this dish, I suggest pairing it with a glass of Godello. This wine, with its crisp, aromatic profile, enhances the rich, earthy notes of the beans and the fresh, oceanic taste of the cockles.

2 tbsp olive oil
125g (4oz) lardons or diced pancetta
1 onion, finely sliced
2 garlic cloves, sliced
1 bay leaf
½ tsp sweet smoked pimentón
1 tbsp tomato purée (paste)
700g (1lb 9oz) jar of white beans
120ml (4fl oz/½ cup) vegetable stock
1kg (2lb 4oz) clams, cleaned
120ml (4fl oz/½ cup) white wine
good handful of flat-leaf parsley, chopped
flaky sea salt and freshly ground black pepper

Heat the oil in a frying pan (skillet) and fry the bacon until it's lightly golden. Add the onion, garlic and bay leaf to the pan and fry for 5–10 minutes until softened.

Add the pimentón, tomato purée and beans with their liquid, and season well with salt and pepper. Add the stock and simmer gently for 5–10 minutes.

Meanwhile, heat a pan over a high heat and add the cockles and wine. Cover and allow to steam for 2–3 minutes until the clams have opened; discard any that do not open. Remove with a slotted spoon to a warm bowl, then add about half of the juices to the beans.

Serve the beans with the clams sprinkled with plenty of parsley.

Tips

Soak the clams in cold salted water for 20 minutes, then drain and soak for 10 minutes in fresh water to help remove any grit before cooking.

You can substitute the clams for cockles.

Braised black beans with spatchcock chicken and herb salsa

- Serves 6
- Takes 2 hours plus overnight soaking

In this recipe, I celebrate the exquisite alubias de Tolosa, a prized variety of small, creamy black beans from the Basque Country, renowned for their rich, earthy flavour. These beans are ideal for slow cooking, absorbing flavours from the stock and aromatics. Paired with succulent roast chicken and complemented by a fresh herb salsa, this dish embodies hearty, rustic simplicity at its best.

1 free-range chicken, spatchcocked
3 tbsp cider vinegar
5 sprigs of lemon thyme
1 bulb garlic, bashed
4 tbsp olive oil
flaky sea salt and freshly ground black pepper

For the beans
400g (14oz) dried Spanish black beans (alubias negra de tolosa)
4 tbsp olive oil
1 onion, finely chopped
3 celery stalks, finely diced
1 bay leaf
600ml (20fl oz/2½ cups) fresh chicken stock

For the salsa
75g (2½oz) flat-leaf parsley
100g (3½oz) basil leaves
1 garlic clove
really good pinch of chilli flakes
50g (2oz/heaped ⅓ cup) blanched almonds
5 tbsp extra virgin olive oil

Start by preparing the beans. Soak the beans in cold water overnight. Drain and rinse, then place in a large saucepan of cold salted water, bring to the boil and simmer gently for 1 hour until tender. Drain.

Heat the olive oil in a casserole dish and fry the onion, celery and bay leaf for 10 minutes, then add the cooked beans and chicken stock. Bring to the boil, then simmer for a further 40 minutes until the beans are really tender and starting to collapse.

Meanwhile, put the chicken in a large dish with the rest of the main ingredients. Season well with salt and pepper and marinate for at least 30 minutes or in the fridge overnight.

Light a lidded barbecue with plenty of charcoal set up for indirect grilling (see Tip) or preheat the oven to 200°C fan (220°C/425°F/gas 7). Place the chicken either on the barbecue with a drip tray with a little water underneath, or in a roasting tin and roast for 1 hour until tender and the skin is golden and crisp.

Meanwhile, blitz the ingredients for the salsa together. Season to taste with salt and pepper and put in a bowl.

Spoon the braised beans onto a large platter. Joint or slice the chicken and place on top of the beans, drizzle with the salsa and serve.

Tip

For indirect grilling, you ned a good pile of long-burning charcoal on either side of your barbecue base and put a drip tray containing a little water in the middle. Light the 2 piles of coal, then put the grilling rack on top, and once hot, you can cook the chicken.

The Spanish Pantry

Beer-braised beef cheeks with smashed white beans

- Serves 4–6
- Takes 4 hours

I normally prepare beef cheeks by braising them in wine or sherry, which beautifully enhances the deep, rich flavours of the meat. However, on this occasion, I experimented with beer as the braising liquid, and I was thrilled with the outcome! While beer is commonly paired with lighter meats, such as chicken or rabbit, I discovered that its malty depth and subtle bitterness complement the robustness of beef cheeks extremely well.

Using beer in this recipe introduces a creative twist, infusing the beef with a complexity that differs from the more traditional wine-based braises. The beer's characteristics permeate the meat, tenderising it while adding layers of nuanced, earthy undertones that elevate the dish. This method results in a dish that is not only rich and mouth-wateringly flavourful but also utterly satisfying and comforting.

This approach to cooking beef cheeks with beer shows the versatility of both the ingredients and the cooking method, offering a fabulous alternative that may just become a new favourite for those looking to explore beyond traditional recipes. Whether for a special dinner or just a cosy meal, these beer-braised beef cheeks provide a deliciously different experience.

Recipe continues overleaf

1.6kg (3lb 8oz) beef cheeks,
    cut into large chunks
2 tbsp plain (all-purpose) flour
4 tbsp olive oil
1 onion, finely sliced
1 carrot, finely chopped
1 celery stalk, finely chopped
3 garlic cloves, finely sliced
1 tbsp tomato purée (paste)
330ml (11¼fl oz/1⅓ cups) Spanish lager
300ml (10fl oz/1¼ cups) fresh beef
    stock
5 sprigs of thyme
2 bay leaves
flaky sea salt and freshly ground
    black pepper

For the beans
4 tbsp extra virgin olive oil, plus extra
    for drizzling
2 garlic cloves, finely sliced
finely grated zest of 1 lemon
2 sprigs of thyme
2 sprigs of rosemary
2 × 400g (14oz) tins of cannellini
    beans, drained and rinsed
1 tbsp cider vinegar

Preheat the oven to 130°C fan (150°C/300°F/gas 2). Season the beef with salt and pepper and dust all over with flour.

Heat half the olive oil in a large, flameproof casserole dish and brown the meat all over, in batches if necessary, then set aside.

Add the rest of the oil to the casserole and gently fry the onion, carrot, celery and garlic for 10 minutes until really soft and fragrant.

Add the tomato purée, beer and stock. Return the beef to the pan along with the herbs and season well with salt and pepper. Bring to the boil, then cover and transfer to the oven and cook for 3 hours until meltingly tender.

For the beans, heat the extra virgin olive oil in a saucepan with the garlic, lemon zest and herbs and warm until fragrant. Add the beans and cook gently for 10 minutes, then remove the large pieces of herb.

Season with salt and pepper, add the vinegar and mash roughly with a fork (add a splash of water if you like a creamier, smoother mash).

Spoon into a warm bowl, drizzle with extra virgin olive oil and sprinkle with plenty of black pepper, then serve with the beef.

Fabada asturiana

- Serves 6
- Takes 2½ hours plus overnight soaking

The best beans for this dish are fabes de la Granja, a traditional variety of white bean from Asturias that is large, tender, and has a creamy texture, making it ideal for the rich and hearty stew. If you can't find them, the closest alternatives are cannellini or butter beans, but true lovers of this dish would agree that nothing quite compares to the authentic *fabes*.

A nice Tempranillo red wine from Toro will go very well indeed, or more classically, a Grenache.

400g (14oz) dried white beans
2 tbsp olive oil
4 pork belly slices
3 cooking chorizo sausages
150g (5oz) morcilla sausages
1 onion, finely chopped
2 garlic cloves, finely sliced
2 sprigs of rosemary
1 tsp smoked hot pimentón
600ml (20fl oz/2½ cups) fresh
   chicken stock
flaky sea salt and freshly ground
   black pepper
crusty bread, to serve

Soak the beans overnight in cold water.

The next day, heat the oil in a saucepan and brown the pork belly, chorizo and morcilla all over. Remove from the pan to a plate.

Add the onion to the pan and cook for 5 minutes, then add the garlic, rosemary and pimentón and cook for a minute more.

Drain the beans and add to the onion pan along with all the browned meat and the chicken stock. Add enough water to make sure all the ingredients are covered. Season well with salt and pepper and bring to the boil, then reduce to a simmer and cook for 1½–2 hours until the beans and meat are tender. Serve with crusty bread.

Pan-fried mackerel with warm roasted tomato and black-eyed bean salad

- Serves 4
- Takes 45 minutes

I've been lucky enough to fish for mackerel in both Norway and Cádiz. The experience couldn't be more different from the ice-cold, crisp waters of Norway to the energetic, warmer shores of Cádiz. In Norway, I had the line-caught mackerel grilled and served with boiled potatoes and a cucumber salad, just simple garnishes that perfectly highlight the fish's fresh flavour. Here, I'm pan-frying the mackerel and pairing it with a warm salad of roasted tomatoes and black-eyed beans. It's a dish that reflects my love for the freshest ingredients and the joy of cooking fish in all its forms.

250g (9oz) cherry tomatoes, halved
2 tbsp olive oil
2 sprigs of rosemary, needles stripped
1 garlic clove, sliced
1 tbsp sherry vinegar
400g (14oz) tin of black-eyed beans, drained and rinsed
4 spring onions (scallions), finely sliced
extra virgin olive oil, for drizzling
4 mackerel, filleted
flaky sea salt and freshly ground black pepper

Preheat the oven to 140°C fan (160°C/320°F/gas 2–3). Drizzle the tomatoes with half the olive oil, scatter with the rosemary and garlic and season well with salt and pepper. Roast for 40 minutes until starting to become dried and sticky.

Add the vinegar and beans and toss together, then add the spring onions and a good glug of extra virgin olive oil.

Meanwhile, drizzle the fish with the rest of the olive oil and season well with salt and pepper, then pan fry for 3–4 minutes on each side until golden and just cooked.

Serve the tomatoes and beans with a piece of mackerel on top and an extra drizzle of extra virgin olive oil.

Warm gigante beans on toast

- Serves 2
- Takes 20 minutes

Sometimes, the simplest dishes bring the most comfort, and beans on toast is a classic example. This elevated version of that classic infuses the humble dish with rich Mediterranean flavours, transforming it into something more special that's perfect for unwinding after a busy day. Featuring warm gigante beans, fragrant herbs and a splash of sherry vinegar for a bright uplift, this recipe offers both a comforting and tasty meal that's ready in just 20 minutes.

4 tbsp olive oil
2 garlic cloves, sliced
1 tsp smoked pimentón
2 tbsp tomato purée (paste)
5 sprigs of oregano
1 sprig of rosemary
2 tbsp sherry vinegar
700g (1lb 9oz) jar of gigante beans, drained
2 slices of bread
extra virgin olive oil, for drizzling
flaky sea salt and freshly ground black pepper

Heat the olive oil in a frying pan (skillet) over a medium heat and gently fry the garlic for a couple of minutes, then add the pimentón, tomato purée, 4 sprigs of oregano, the rosemary and vinegar and bubble for a minute before adding the beans and plenty of salt and pepper. Cook for 3–4 minutes until the beans are hot.

Toast the bread and drizzle with extra virgin olive oil, then spoon the beans onto the toast. Drizzle with more extra virgin olive oil, garnish with oregano leaves and plenty of pepper and serve.

The Spanish Pantry

Sopa de alubias with mojo verde

- Serves 6
- Takes 30 minutes

On a brisk day, there's nothing quite as comforting as a bowl of creamy, hearty soup. This particular recipe not only warms you from the inside out, but also brings a fantastic burst of energising, uplifting flavour, thanks to the vibrant green mojo verde sauce. The sauce, with its zingy garlic and coriander, adds a tang that makes the soup utterly satisfying and leaves you wanting more.

If you find yourself without the fresh herbs needed for the mojo verde, don't worry – the soup is equally delicious served simply with some crusty bread. However, if you are able, the mojo verde is well worth the effort, as it totally transforms the soup.

3 tbsp olive oil
1 onion, finely chopped
2 garlic cloves, crushed
2 tsp sweet pimentón
small pinch of saffron threads
    soaked in 2tbsp just boiled water
    for 5 minutes
1 bay leaf
2 × 700g (1lb 9oz) jars of Spanish
    white beans (alubias blancas)
800ml (28fl oz/3½ cups) fresh
    chicken or vegetable stock
flaky sea salt and freshly ground
    black pepper
crusty bread, to serve

For the mojo verde
50g (2oz) flat-leaf parsley
30g (1oz) coriander (cilantro)
20g (¾oz) chives
2 guindilla peppers, finely chopped
2 garlic cloves, crushed
1 tsp ground cumin
2 tbsp sherry vinegar
75–100ml (2½–3½fl oz/scant ⅓–½ cup)
    extra virgin olive oil

Heat the olive oil in a saucepan and gently fry the onion for 5 minutes, then add the garlic, pimentón, saffron and bay leaf. Blend half the beans into a paste and add to the pan. Fry for a minute, then add the stock, plenty of seasoning and the rest of the beans. Reduce to a simmer and cook for 10 minutes.

For the mojo verde, blitz the herbs, guindilla and garlic in a small food processor. Add the cumin and vinegar and blitz again, season with salt and pepper, then stir in the extra virgin olive oil until you have a thick, spoonable sauce.

Spoon the soup into bowls, spoon over the mojo verde and serve with the crusty bread.

Aubergine and bean dip

- Serves 6–8
- Takes 1 hour

Enjoying this gorgeous dip sitting outside Iris, our home in Andalusia, watching the sunset with a glass of Amontillado in hand, is a spiritual experience. When I prepare this dip with tahini instead of yoghurt, it transforms into a brilliant vegan treat. It certainly enhanced the joy of overlooking the waters towards Tangier from my home. It really shows the versatility and richness that beans can bring to our diet, providing texture, nourishment and depth to so many recipes.

The combination of creamy, smoky roasted aubergine with the hearty beans creates a simple but satisfying snack. This dip is all about the flavours best enjoyed with home-made tortilla chips or crudités. A good Amontillado is the perfect accompaniment.

1 aubergine (eggplant)
1 tbsp olive oil
700g (1lb 9oz) jar of gigante
    or butter (lima) beans, drained
2 garlic cloves, crushed
1 tsp ground cumin
good pinch of smoked hot pimentón
3–4 tbsp extra virgin olive oil
1 tbsp thick plain or Greek yoghurt
squeeze of lemon juice
flaky sea salt and freshly ground
    black pepper
crisps, tortilla chips or crudités,
    to serve

Preheat the oven to 170°C fan (190°C/375°F/gas 5).

Rub the aubergine in olive oil, pierce with a knife in several places and place in a small roasting tin. Roast for 40–45 minutes until really tender and squishy. Allow to cool enough to handle.

Scoop the insides out of the aubergine into a food processor and add the beans, garlic, spices and extra virgin olive oil. Whiz together, then add the yoghurt and whiz again. Add lemon juice and salt and pepper to taste, then serve with crisps, tortilla chips or crudités.

Broad beans braised in olive oil

- Makes 2 × 500g (1lb 2oz) jars
- Takes 30 minutes

I want to explain how to store broad beans in jars for the year. This dish is a celebration of spring, capturing the essence of the season in every jar. In Spain, particularly in Extremadura, the broad bean season is famously fleeting, humorously said to 'start in April and finish in April'. The brief window of peak freshness is eagerly anticipated, as these beans are best when harvested young, at about 5cm (2in) long, tender enough to eat without the need for podding.

Broad beans are incredibly bountiful, often producing more than can be immediately consumed, making preservation an essential practice. This not only extends their shelf life but also allows us to enjoy their delicate flavour throughout the whole year. Preserved in jars with aromatic olive oil and a blend of herbs and spices, these beans transform into a favourite pantry item, ready to enhance all sorts of meals with their fresh, springtime taste. The oil is great for dipping.

1 kg (2lb 4oz) small fresh broad bean pods
200ml (7fl oz/scant 1 cup) olive oil
2 garlic cloves, bashed
pared zest of 1 lemon
1 tsp coriander seeds
½ tsp black peppercorns
2 tbsp apple vinegar
1 tsp flaky sea salt
large handful of soft herbs of your choice (tarragon, thyme, marjoram, basil, mint)
50–75ml (2½fl oz/scant ⅓ cup) extra virgin olive oil
flaky sea salt and freshly ground black pepper

Pod the beans and plunge into boiling water for 3–4 minutes, then drain and refresh immediately under cold running water. If you like, you can now slip off the tougher outer skin but if the beans are nice and young you can leave them as they are.

Warm the olive oil with the garlic, lemon zest, coriander seeds and peppercorns over a low heat for 3–4 minutes, then set aside to cool and infuse.

Put the beans in a bowl and toss with the vinegar, salt, herbs and extra virgin olive oil, then transfer into sealable, sterilised jars. Pour over the infused oil so that it covers the beans completely, and close with the lid.

Bring a large pan of water to the boil and place the sealed jars into the water so they are submerged. Boil for 15–20 minutes. Carefully remove from the water and leave to cool. You will hear them pop as the air seals in the jars and the lid indents pop in. Store in a cool dark place for up to a year

Jamón

Growing up, the family pig was much more than just another animal, it was part of our daily life, and a way of making sure nothing ever went to waste. Pigs were nature's organic recyclers; they turned kitchen scraps, leftover vegetables, and even garden trimmings, into food that would keep us going through the whole year. Although this can be difficult for some to understand in the context of modern-day convenience, this was deep, rural Spain, and life could be tough – so nothing was ever wasted. The pigs ate what we didn't, they lived good lives, were well tended and, in return, they gave us everything from jamón to sausages.

A much-awaited and special moment in the annual calendar of village life was the *matanza*, the big day, when the whole extended family and friends gathered to turn all their hard work into something that would last and that we'd share for the whole year. This was a time of coming together, and in processing the animal, we'd ensure that every part of the pig would have a purpose, nothing ever wasted. I remember my dad teaching me an important life lesson from this, too. He used the symbolism of all parts having a purpose to help me understand the importance of everyone's equally important roles in life. 'In work,' he'd say, 'whatever you do, do it to the best of your ability. Everyone has a different but important part to play.'

Once the legs were properly salted and hung in the cellar, it felt like a reward. It was an art form that taught us a vital life lesson about delayed gratification. I loved going down to check on the hams, watching them change bit by bit. The cellar would fill with that rich, smoky scent, coming from the chorizo that were curing at the same time, and I'd feel proud, knowing that those now-beautiful jamónes represented all the effort, care and time we'd put in.

To me, every slice of jamón still brings back those memories. It's more than just food, it's something to be savoured and appreciated. It's a reminder of family, of taking care over food production and preparation, and of a way of life where nothing ever went to waste. It's the taste of tradition of making the most of what you have, and of the simple joy in seeing hard work turn into something special.

Fried potatoes with jamón Ibérico, prawns and crispy eggs

- Serves 4
- Takes 1 hour

Huevos fritos rotos is the Spanish name for this dish and 'broken fried eggs' is a dish that people absolutely love. It's a thoroughly rustic, profoundly satisfying medley of textures and flavours – crispy, velvety and rich. At its heart are fried eggs and sumptuous jamón Ibérico.

At Pizarro, we get creative and elevate this dish by adding king prawns sautéed in garlic and chilli for an incredible depth of flavour. For this recipe, we've kept it simple with just jamón Ibérico and juicy prawns.

A crisp, cold beer or refreshing cider is all that's needed with this stunning classic.

700ml (24fl oz/3½ cups) olive oil, plus extra for frying the eggs
700g (1lb 9oz) floury potatoes, peeled and cut into thin chips
300g (10½oz) large raw shell-on prawns (shrimp)
120g (4oz) jamón Ibérico
4 medium free-range eggs
flaky sea salt and freshly ground black pepper

Heat the oil in a deep sauté pan until shimmering and around 140°C (280°F). Add the potatoes and fry for 5 minutes until translucent but not coloured. Scoop out with a slotted spoon onto paper towels.

Increase the heat of the large pan of oil to 180°C (350°F), add the potatoes and fry for 3–4 minutes until golden and crispy all over. Remove with a slotted spoon, drain on paper towels and season with salt.

Plunge the prawns into boiling water until just pink then drain immediately.

Finally, heat 3 tablespoons of oil in a frying pan (skillet) and crack in the eggs and allow them to bubble, spooning the hot oil over the top, cooking for barely a minute until the whites are starting to crisp but the yolks are still runny.

Scoop out with a slotted spoon and drain on paper towels. Serve the crispy patatas scattered with the jamón and the juicy prawns, with an egg on top and a scattering of sea salt and freshly ground black pepper.

The Spanish Pantry

Jamón serrano and watermelon salad with honey and basil

- Serves 4
- Takes 25 minutes

Growing up, watermelons from our family garden were the highlight of summer. These were small and incredibly sweet, perfect for refreshing dishes like this serrano ham and watermelon salad. This recipe rekindles my most cherished childhood memories and is easy to recreate using simple, fresh ingredients, transforming them into a visually impressive and delicious summer dish.

For an exciting twist at your next summer barbecue, try grilling the watermelon slices. This method intensifies the fruit's natural sweetness and imparts a subtle, smoky flavour, which pairs with the salty richness of the serrano ham. The combination of smoky, sweet watermelon and savoury ham creates a blend of flavours and aromas that captivates as well as delights the senses.

1 baby watermelon
200g (7oz) jamón serrano
juice of 1 lime
1 tbsp honey
good pinch of chilli flakes
3 tbsp extra virgin olive oil
large handful of basil leaves
flaky sea salt and freshly ground
   black pepper

Remove the skin from the watermelon, cut the flesh into small wedges and arrange on a platter.

Arrange the jamón serrano around the watermelon and squeeze over the lime juice. Season with salt and pepper, drizzle over the honey and scatter with the chilli flakes.

Finally, drizzle with extra virgin olive oil, scatter with basil and serve immediately.

Tip

You can make this a bit more substantial by adding a bag of wild rocket (arugula) or other baby leaves, if you like.

The Spanish Pantry

Jamón, peach and pistachio

- Serves 4
- Takes 30 minutes

This salad is a perfect summer dish, one we especially love to enjoy at Iris, Cádiz.

Pistachios have recently become a favourite in Spain, growing especially well in regions like Castilla-La Mancha and Andalusia, where the warm climate helps them thrive. Known for their vibrant green colour and rich, nutty flavour, Spanish pistachios can add a special touch to traditional and modern dishes, and importantly, they have become an economic boost for various smaller communities.

Jamón Ibérico Cinco Jotas is the perfect addition here, its exquisite flavour elevating the dish and complementing the other ingredients beautifully. I think goats' cheese is perfect for this dish, but you can also use Requesón (page 130), which pairs just as well with the sweet, juicy peaches and savoury jamón. The infused milk adds a lovely depth of flavour, bringing everything together harmoniously – ideal for a warm, sunny lunch. Happy summer!

1 tbsp olive oil
4 ripe peaches, halved
2 sprigs of marjoram
1 tbsp honey
2 tbsp Pedro Ximénez sherry vinegar
125g (4oz) jamón Ibérico
60g (2oz) shelled pistachios
100g (3½oz) soft goats' cheese
2 tbsp extra virgin olive oil
flaky sea salt and freshly ground
    black pepper

Heat the olive oil in a non-stick frying pan (skillet) over a medium–high heat. Add the peaches, cut-side down, and cook for 2–3 minutes until just starting to colour.

Add the marjoram, honey and sherry vinegar and some salt and pepper and continue to cook for a further 2–3 minutes until sticky and tender. Flip over and turn off the heat.

Arrange the jamón on a serving platter. Toast the pistachios in a dry frying pan (skillet) until lightly charred and fragrant, then roughly chop.

Add the peaches to the platter and spoon over any juices from the pan. Scatter with the goats' cheese and pistachios and drizzle with the extra virgin olive oil to serve.

Roasted razor clams with crispy jamón serrano

- Serves 4
- Takes 20 minutes plus soaking

Razor clams are a must-buy for me whenever I see them at the market in Barbate. In Cádiz and other parts of Spain, razor clams are hand-harvested along sandy beaches and shallow waters. Fishermen use an old technique of sprinkling a bit of salt or gently pouring water over the clam's burrow. This makes the clam rise to the surface, so it's easy to catch without harming the environment. Whenever I prepare them, this memory of watching the fisherman catch them in this age-old way comes back to me.

Here in the South the clams are smaller, so you can enjoy them whole. But if you get the bigger ones, it's best to cut away the black part, which contains the digestive tract, as it can taste gritty and a little bitter. I would recommend a lovely buttery Chardonnay with this dish, to take you to seventh heaven!

1kg (2lb 4oz) small razor clams
2 tbsp olive oil
2 garlic cloves, finely sliced
good pinch of chilli flakes
5 sprigs of oregano, leaves stripped
8 slices of jamón serrano
juice of 1 lemon
handful of flat-leaf parsley, finely chopped

Soak the razor clams in salted water for 30 minutes, then run under cold water to make sure they are clean of seaweed.

Preheat the oven to 200°C fan (220°C/425°F/gas 7).

Put the clams in a single layer in a roasting tin and drizzle with the oil, then scatter with the garlic, chilli and oregano. Lay the jamón serrano on top and roast for 5 minutes, then turn the tray around and roast for a further 5 minutes until the clams are all open and the jamón serrano is crispy. Discard any clams that remain closed.

Squeeze over the lemon juice and scatter with parsley to serve.

Tip

When eating, cut away the black bit that contains the digestive tract as this can be gritty and bitter.

Spanish egg and jamón butty

- Serves 4
- Takes 30 minutes

I love great sandwiches – and if you're a fan of egg and bacon, you're going to love this as much as I do. The crispy, salty jamón creates a whole range of flavours, and with the garlic kick from the alioli, it's heaven in a bite. The pimentón adds a touch of smokiness that takes me right back home, which in my opinion, takes this butty to the next level. I love my bubbles with this, so a glass of cava or an effervescent beer go perfectly.

4 small rolls or ciabatta
100ml (3½fl oz/scant ½ cup) olive oil
4 medium free-range eggs
12 slices of jamón serrano
good pinch of pimentón
2–4 tbsp Fermented spiced
   Spanish ketchup (page 38)
   or regular ketchup (optional)

For the alioli
2 free-range egg yolks
2 tsp cider vinegar
1 garlic clove, grated or crushed
200–250ml (7½fl oz/1 cup) olive oil
2 tbsp extra virgin olive oil
lemon juice, to taste
flaky sea salt and freshly ground
   black pepper

To make the alioli, whisk the egg yolks with the vinegar and garlic and season well with salt and pepper. Gradually whisk in the olive oils until you have a thick, glossy mayonnaise. Season to taste with lemon juice.

Slice the bread in half and brush with some of the olive oil. Heat a grill (broiler) to medium–high and toast the bread until lightly golden.

Heat a little of the olive oil in a large non-stick frying pan (skillet) and fry the jamón serrano until it is crispy and golden. Remove to a warm plate.

Add the rest of the olive oil to the pan and heat until it shimmers, then crack in the eggs and use a spoon to coat the top of the eggs so they puff up and turn crispy and golden. Cook for no more than a minute, then remove and drain on paper towels. Season with salt, pepper and a good pinch of pimentón.

Spread the toast with some alioli and some fermented ketchup, if you like, then top with the jamón serrano and crispy egg and and serve.

The Spanish Pantry

Jamón, bread and egg soup

- Serves 6
- Takes 30 minutes

For me, this might just be the best soup ever. It's filled with memories, flavours and pure happiness – maybe that sounds a bit sentimental, but it's true. This soup has been a favourite at my mum's house since I can remember, and in our family for generations. It's made with just a few simple ingredients. I always have stock at home so I have used it in this recipe, but you don't even need it – the jamón and garlic give you all the rich flavours you'll need. Enjoy with a glass of Oloroso sherry.

2 tbsp olive oil
200g (7oz) jamón, cut into pieces
3 garlic cloves, finely sliced
1 tsp smoked sweet pimentón
1 bay leaf
150g (5oz) slightly stale bread, torn into chunks
1 litre (34fl oz/4 cups) fresh chicken stock
2 large free-range eggs, lightly beaten
flaky sea salt and freshly ground black pepper

Heat the oil in a frying pan (skillet) and fry the jamón for a few minutes, then add the garlic, pimentón and bay leaf. Add the bread and allow it to brown lightly in the oil.

Add the stock and cook until the bread has broken down and the stock thickened.

Pour the eggs into the simmering soup in a stream, stirring lightly so they form ribbons. Season with salt and pepper to taste and serve.

Braised jamón and pork knuckle with olive oil mash

- Serves 6
- Takes 3½ hours

This might not be a traditional Spanish dish, but I love serving it when people come over as it's perfect for sharing.

Fried jamón really makes this dish special, adding a rich, savoury flavour that blends perfectly with the rest of the ingredients. The olive oil mash is just right for soaking up the sauce and tender meat.

A fresh green salad with a light vinaigrette also helps balance all the richness. Just mix some extra virgin olive oil, a splash of sherry vinegar or lemon juice, a pinch of salt and a dash of Dijon mustard for a simple, zesty dressing. Toss it with the greens, and you've got the perfect fresh side to keep everything feeling light and delicious.

4 tbsp olive oil
200g (7oz) jamón, sliced
1 large onion, finely sliced
2 celery stalks, finely chopped
1 carrot, finely chopped
4 garlic cloves, crushed
2 pork knuckles
2 bay leaves
2 tsp smoked sweet pimentón
150ml (5fl oz/scant ⅔ cup) white wine
200g (7oz) tomatoes, chopped
300ml (10fl oz/1¼ cups) fresh chicken
    stock
flaky sea salt and freshly ground
    black pepper

For the mash
800g (1lb 12oz) potatoes, cut into
    chunks
2 garlic cloves, peeled
100ml (3½fl oz/scant ½ cup) extra
    virgin olive oil

Preheat the oven to 140°C fan (160°C/320°F/gas 2–3).

Heat the olive oil in a flameproof casserole dish and fry the jamón until lightly browned.

Add the onion, celery, carrot and garlic and fry for 10 minutes, then add the pork to the pan along with the bay leaves, pimentón and wine and bubble for 5 minutes.

Add the tomatoes and stock and season well with salt and pepper. Bring to the boil, then reduce to a simmer. Cover and cook in the oven for 3 hours until the knuckle is starting to fall apart. Remove the knuckle from the pan, remove and discard the skin and fat, then shred the meat (discarding the bone) and return the meat to the sauce.

For the mash, put the potatoes and garlic in a pan of cold salted water and bring to the boil. Reduce to a simmer and cook for 15–20 minutes until very tender. Drain, reserving a cup 250ml (8½fl oz) of the cooking water, and return the potatoes to the dry pan over a low heat. Mash and then add in the extra virgin olive oil and enough of the reserved cooking water and mash until rich and creamy. Season with salt and pepper to taste and serve with the braised jamón and pork.

Tip

You could also make this with ham hock instead of knuckle.

Saffron

Saffron is the star wherever it appears, adding a warm, earthy depth that transforms each dish. Saffron's unique flavour and aroma bring a touch of luxury, proving why this spice has been cherished for centuries. People think that saffron is expensive, but actually this is not accurate because just a few stems will go a long way.

Saffron has been a treasured part of Spain's history and cuisine for hundreds of years, adding not only flavour but also a sense of tradition to many of Spain's most beloved dishes. Brought to Spain by the Moors around the 8th century, saffron found its preferred home in the fields of La Mancha, where the warm, dry climate allowed it to thrive. This 'red gold', as it's known, is still hand-harvested today, a delicate and time-consuming process that involves picking each crocus flower's tiny red stigmas by hand – a practice that preserves both the quality and heritage of Spanish saffron – and carefully drying them.

In many Spanish kitchens, saffron has a special role, especially in classic dishes like paella, where it gives the rice its famous golden colour and warm, earthy flavour. While people occasionally use a yellow food colouring to give paella the traditional hue, it can never match the true taste and aroma of real saffron. I've noticed among some Brit friends and people who are not particularly familiar with saffron, a little palate education is needed. Once you've tasted high-quality Spanish saffron and your taste buds have met it properly, you'll forever recognise its luxuriously earthy undertones and the subtle floral sweetness that lingers and resonates across the palate, and you'll even miss it when it's not there.

I've been lucky enough to attend the Saffron Rose Festival in Consuegra, La Mancha, where I had the chance to pick the highly regarded saffron myself. This unforgettable experience gave me a deep appreciation for the spice, seeing first-hand the dedication and skill involved in bringing saffron from field to kitchen. The festival itself is filled with vibrant colours, lively music and, of course, the unmistakable aroma of saffron in the air.

Floretas

- Serves 6
- Takes 30 minutes plus resting and infusing

The name of this dish comes from the Spanish word *flores*, meaning 'flowers'. They're a highly popular treat in my area, always making an appearance on the table on special occasions. Traditionally, we enjoy them on their own, from breakfast all the way through to a mid-morning coffee.

This version was created especially for my restaurant José by Pizarro in Abu Dhabi, incorporating local honey and saffron to give it a unique regional twist. The delicate sweetness of the honey and the aromatic saffron elevate the flavours, making it a delightful combination of familiar, traditional and local ingredients in the UEA.

125ml (4fl oz/½ cup) water
pared zest of 1 lemon
1 tbsp honey, plus extra for drizzling
2 star anise
150g (5oz/scant 1¼ cups) plain (all-purpose) flour
2 free-range eggs
2 tsp olive oil
75ml (2½fl oz/scant ⅓ cup) whole milk
500ml (17fl oz/2 cups) olive oil, for deep-frying

For the custard
450ml (15¾fl oz/scant 2 cups) whole milk
good pinch of saffron threads
2 free-range egg yolks
20g (¾oz/scant ¼ cup) cornflour (cornstarch)
2 tbsp caster (superfine) sugar
3 tbsp double (heavy) cream

Put the water in a saucepan with the lemon zest, honey and star anise and bring to the boil, then set aside to infuse until cold.

Put the flour into a bowl and make a well in the middle. Crack the eggs into the well, add the 2 teaspoons of olive oil and start to stir and incorporate the flour, adding the infused water a little at a time until you have a smooth batter. Stir in the milk and set aside for at least 30 minutes.

To make the custard, warm the milk with the saffron, then leave to infuse for 10 minutes. Beat the egg yolks with the cornflour and sugar, then pour over the infused milk and whisk together. Return the mixture to the pan with the cream and heat over a low heat, stirring until the mixture has thickened.

Bring the 500ml (17fl oz/2 cups) of olive oil to 170°C (340°F) in a deep, heavy-based pan. Dip your floreta mould into the oil to heat, dab on paper towels, then dip into the batter, filling not quite to the top. Then dip it back into the hot oil and allow to cook for 1–2 minutes until golden and crisp. Ease off the mould, then remove from the oil with a slotted spoon onto a plate lined with paper towels. Repeat until you have made all 6 floretas. Divide the custard between 6 bowls, then top with a few floretas drizzled with honey.

Tip

There is no real substitute for a floreta mould – a flower-shaped mould on a long stick – but they are easy to find online.

The Spanish Pantry

Deep-fried cauliflower bites with saffron sauce

- Serves 4–6
- Takes 45 minutes

This recipe is a modern twist on a dish my mum makes for Easter. She often uses more ingredients and batters cauliflower with salted cod and boiled egg, simmering it in a garlic and bay leaf sauce. It's a homely mix of flavours that's close to my heart, especially because my mum makes it so lovingly. In my chef's version here, I deep-fry the cauliflower for a crisp texture and use a rich saffron sauce, making it perfect for a canapé party, or to enjoy as *pica-pica* – a buffet of small dishes.

Cauliflower may seem humble, but it's a vegetable with a story and has been loved for centuries. It originated in the Eastern Mediterranean and spread across Europe in the Middle Ages. In Spain, we've mastered the art of bringing out the best to use in many flavourful classic dishes. For a really simple approach, you can blanch the cauliflower, then fry it with garlic, chilli, lemon and, of course, plenty of extra virgin olive oil!

Enjoy with a glass of bubbles for extra refinement.

750ml (26fl oz/generous 3 cups) olive oil
1 cauliflower, leaves separated and head broken into florets
75g (2½oz/⅔ cup) plain (all-purpose) flour
good pinch of smoked sweet pimentón
1 tsp ground cumin
2 large free-range eggs, beaten
flaky sea salt and freshly ground black pepper

For the sauce
2 large free-range eggs
3 tbsp olive oil
2 garlic cloves, finely sliced
1 bay leaf
200ml (7fl oz/scant 1 cup) fresh vegetable or chicken stock
pinch of saffron threads
4 tbsp double (heavy) cream

To make the sauce, put the eggs into a saucepan of cold water and bring to the boil, then cook for 6 minutes. Drain, then refresh under cold water.

Heat the oil in a large saucepan and gently fry the garlic and bay leaf over a low heat until fragrant. Peel the eggs, mash the yolks and chop the whites into small pieces. Add the yolks to the pan, then gradually add the stock, whisking. Add the saffron and salt and pepper and leave to simmer for 10 minutes until thickened.

Add the cream and chopped egg whites and set aside.

To make the cauliflower, heat the oil in a deep-sided, heavy-based pan until it reaches 180°C (350°F).

Blanch the cauliflower florets in a pan of boiling water for 1–2 minutes, then drain well. Toss them with the flour, pimentón, cumin and plenty of seasoning so they are coated all over. Toss in the beaten egg, then fry in batches for 2–3 minutes until golden brown and crispy. Drain on paper towels and season with salt.

Warm the sauce, spoon into shallow bowls and top with the crispy golden cauliflower to serve.

Saffron and prawn croquetas

- Makes about 30
- Takes 1 hour plus chilling

Croquetas are surprisingly easy to make, despite what many people think. They're one of those dishes that let you experiment with flavours in a fun way. Each time I make them, I'm inspired to try new combinations! As a special treat for you, dear reader, I've gone with the delicate sweetness of prawns and distinctive saffron, adding a little bit of luxury to these delicious bites.

700ml (24fl oz/3 cups) whole milk
good pinch of saffron threads
2 tbsp just-boiled water
100g (3½oz) unsalted butter
120g (4oz/scant 1 cup) plain
    (all-purpose) flour, plus 2 tbsp extra
1 tbsp olive oil
250g (9oz) raw king prawns (shrimp)
2 garlic cloves, finely sliced
good pinch of chilli flakes
2 free-range eggs, beaten
150g (5oz/1 cup) panko breadcrumbs
1 litre (34fl oz/4 cups) light olive or
    vegetable oil, for frying
flaky sea salt and freshly ground
    black pepper

Heat the milk gently in a saucepan. Mix the saffron with the just-boiled water. Line a baking tin with clingfilm (plastic wrap).

Melt the butter in a separate pan, add the flour and cook for 2–3 minutes, stirring. Gradually add the milk, stirring continuously, until you have a smooth, very thick béchamel sauce. Add the saffron and its water and cook for a further 1–2 minutes, then set aside.

In a frying pan (skillet), heat the oil and add the prawns, garlic and chilli flakes. Season with salt and pepper and cook until the prawns are just pink. Remove from the pan and roughly chop. Add to the béchamel and mix together. Pour into the prepared baking tin and chill until cold.

Take spoonfuls of the mix and roll into balls about 30g (1oz) each. Put the 2 tablespoons of flour in a dish and the beaten egg and breadcrumbs in 2 more.

Coat each of the balls in flour, then beaten egg and then breadcrumbs. Place on a baking sheet and, when they are all done, freeze for 1 hour.

When ready to cook, heat the oil to 170°C (340°F). Drop a few of the croquetas into the oil and fry for 3–4 minutes until deep golden and hot to the middle. Remove with a slotted spoon and drain on paper towels while you fry the rest. Serve straight away.

The Spanish Pantry

Saffron and honey torrijas

- Serves 4
- Takes 25 minutes

I often joke that I'm sweet enough, but when it comes to desserts, I can't resist indulging in a beautifully made torrija. This classic Spanish dish is essentially about transforming simple ingredients into something sublime, and it all starts with the milk infusion. Infusing milk with different things not only enhances the overall taste but brings the humble torrija to life.

In this recipe, I've chosen to infuse the milk with a trio of amazing flavours: saffron, cardamom and orange. Saffron, a spice I adore and frequently use in my ice cream recipes, adds a luxurious richness here as well. The warm, earthy undertones of the saffron blend perfectly with the aromatic zest of the orange, while cardamom introduces a subtle, spicy complexity that transforms the dish.

400ml (13fl oz/generous 1½ cups) whole milk
good pinch of saffron threads
50g (2oz/heaped ¼ cup) caster (superfine) sugar, plus extra for dusting
2 tbsp honey
4 cardamom pods, cracked open
pared zest of 1 orange
4 thick slices of slightly stale bread
2 large free-range eggs, beaten
100ml (3½fl oz/scant ½ cup) olive oil

Put the milk in a saucepan with the saffron, sugar, honey, cardamom and pared orange zest. Gently heat and infuse for about 10 minutes until the sugar has all dissolved. Remove from the heat and leave to stand for 10 minutes to infuse.

Pour the milk into a large dish and dip in the bread slices so they are soaked in the flavoured milk but not saturated and falling apart.

Beat the eggs in a separate shallow dish, then dip the soaked bread into the egg.

Heat the oil in a large, non-stick frying pan and fry the bread for 2–3 minutes on each side until golden brown. Drain on a plate lined with paper towels and dust with caster sugar. Arrange on plates and serve.

Saffron monkfish nuggets with saffron alioli

- Serves 4–6
- Takes 30 minutes plus marinating

These are no ordinary nuggets – instead, they are a celebration of Southern Spanish cuisine, transformed into what might just be the ultimate bite-sized delights. Inspired by the traditional dish *cazón en adobo*, in which dogfish is marinated and enjoyed for its hearty and flavourful character, this recipe introduces a similar concept but with a unique twist, using monkfish to create a gourmet version of everyone's favourite comfort food.

I would simply have a very cold beer with these gorgeous nuggets.

700g (1lb 9oz) monkfish tail, cut into bite-sized pieces
1 tsp cumin seeds
good pinch of saffron threads
2 tbsp just-boiled water
pinch of smoked sweet pimentón
1 bay leaf
1 tbsp sherry vinegar
120ml (4fl oz/½ cup) white wine
100g (3½oz/heaped ¾ cup) plain (all-purpose) flour
1 large free-range egg, beaten
125g (4oz/2½ cups) panko breadcrumbs
750ml (26fl oz/generous 1 cup) olive oil, for deep-frying
flaky sea salt and freshly ground black or white pepper
lemon wedges, to serve

For the alioli
pinch of saffron threads
1 tbsp just-boiled water
2 free-range egg yolks
2 tsp cider vinegar
200–250ml (7–8½fl oz/1 cup) olive oil
2 tbsp extra virgin olive oil
lemon juice, to taste

Put the monkfish in a bowl with the cumin seeds. Put the saffron in a small bowl, pour over the just-boiled water and leave to stand for a few minutes. Pour this into the dish and add the pimentón, bay leaf, vinegar and white wine. Leave to marinate for 20 minutes.

To make the alioli, put the saffron in a small bowl, pour over the just-boiled water and leave to stand for a few minutes.

Put the egg yolks in a bowl with some salt and pepper and whisk in the cider vinegar.

Gradually whisk in the olive oil until you have a smooth, thick emulsion, then whisk in the extra virgin olive oil. Add the saffron water and lemon juice to taste and set aside.

Remove the fish from the marinade and pat dry. Season the flour with salt and pepper, then coat the fish in the flour, then in the egg and finally the panko breadcrumbs.

Heat the oil to 170°C (340°F) in a deep-sided pan and fry the nuggets for 3–4 minutes until golden and just cooked. Sprinkle with salt and serve with the alioli and a good squeeze of lemon.

Saffron salt with seared scallops

- Serves 2
- Takes 20 minutes

People sometimes pull my leg because I've got a thing about salt. For a dish this simple, high-quality salt makes all the difference. Here, we're using sea salt from Puerto de Santa María, near our home, Iris, where the salt is harvested straight from the Atlantic. This salt isn't just incredible in flavour, it's also rich in essential minerals like magnesium, calcium and potassium that bring both depth and good health. Good salt transforms a dish, enhancing the natural flavours without overpowering them. The complex minerality of Puerto de Santa María's sea salt adds a briny touch, making the saffron and scallops sing in a way that using ordinary table salt just can't achieve.

Salt from Añana is another of my favourites, coming from the Basque country, sourced from ancient salt springs. Unlike sea salt, Añana salt comes from mineral-rich underground springs that flow into shallow pools to naturally evaporate under the sun.

I recommend a glass of cold manzanilla sherry with these scallops because of the exquisite dry, saltiness.

100g (3½oz) flaky sea salt
pinch of saffron threads
10 fresh scallops
1 tbsp olive oil
3 very fresh garlic cloves, finely sliced
75ml (2½fl oz/scant ⅓ cup) extra virgin olive oil

Use a clean coffee or spice grinder to grind half the salt and saffron to a pale lemon yellow, then use your fingers to add the rest of the salt and saffron and rub together to create a lovely sprinkly texture. Tip into a pot with a lid to keep for future recipes.

Pat the scallops dry, then toss in the olive oil. Heat a pan over a high heat and sear the scallops for a minute on each side until golden and just cooked. Transfer to a plate. Add the garlic and extra virgin olive oil to the hot pan and let the garlic infuse, then spoon over the scallops. Scatter with a good pinch of saffron salt and serve.

Saffron flan

- Serves 6–8
- Takes 1 hour plus chilling

Crème caramel is a favourite in all my restaurants as well as in my family. I remember as a child, my mum would always make flan for the weekend, and the wonderful flavours of fresh milk and eggs from our farm are still strong in my memory. Funnily enough, I remember being a bit envious of my friends whose parents bought flans from the shops – I loved the bubbles in those flans; they looked so appealing, even though I preferred the flavour of my mum's homemade flan.

These days, I add saffron to enhance the flavours with that extra dimension, bringing a new depth to this classic dessert. In the restaurants, I also whip a bit of cream with a touch of Pedro Ximénez sherry vinegar. This adds a lovely balance, cutting through the richness of the eggs and giving the dish a lovely finish.

pinch of saffron threads
150g (5oz/heaped ¾ cup) caster (superfine) sugar
3 tbsp water
397g (14oz) tin of condensed milk
400ml (13fl oz/generous 1½ cups) whole milk
3 large free-range eggs
1 free-range egg yolk
2 tsp vanilla bean paste
Almendrados (page 106), to serve (optional)

Preheat the oven to 150°C fan (170°C/330°F/gas 3) and boil a large kettle of water.

Mix the saffron with 1 tablespoon of hot water and set aside.

In a saucepan, melt the sugar with the water until melted, then increase the heat and bubble, without stirring, until you have a lovely golden caramel. Pour into a 20cm (8in) ovenproof dish and swirl to coat, then leave to cool.

Whisk the condensed milk, milk, eggs, egg yolk and vanilla in a large jug until smooth, then whisk in the saffron water. Pour over the caramel, then place in a large roasting tin in the middle of the oven. Pour boiling water around the outside of the dish so it comes about halfway up the sides, then cook for 40–45 minutes until it is set but with a slight wobble.

Remove from the oven and cool, then chill for at least 3 hours.

Run a sharp knife around the outside of the dish and invert onto a plate with a lip. You will feel a satisfying plop when it releases and the caramel floods the plate. Serve with the almendrados, if you like.

The Spanish Pantry

Spanish daisy cocktail

- Makes 1
- Takes 10 minutes

After a long and productive day of shooting for this book in Iris, we fancied a nice drink and decided to experiment with a cocktail using saffron. We infused some tequila overnight, and by the next day, the tequila alone was incredible. Try it with a slice of orange and a dash of ground cinnamon as you will do with the lemon and salt – it's heavenly! Knowing how well saffron pairs with citrus, we came up with a twist on the classic Daisy cocktail, creating the Spanish daisy cocktail, which turned out to be perfect!

ice cubes
50ml (1¾fl oz/3 tbsp)
    saffron-infused tequila (see Tip)
1 tbsp lemon juice
1 tbsp Curaçao, Grand Marnier
    or other orange liqueur
2 tsp caster (superfine) sugar
tiny pinch of flaky sea salt
splash of soda water
tiny pinch of saffron strands,
    to garnish

For the rim (optional):
1 lemon wedge
1 tbsp fine sea salt
1 tbsp caster (superfine) sugar

Fill a shaker with ice and mix together the tequila, lemon juice, orange liqueur, sugar and salt, then shake well.

If adding the garnish, rub your lemon wedge along the rim of a chilled cocktail glass. Combine the salt and sugar together on a plate, then dip the rim of your glass into the mixture.

Strain into a chilled cocktail glass, top up with a splash of soda, garnish with saffron strands and serve.

Tip

To make your own saffron tequila, put 2–3g (⅛ oz) of saffron in a small muslin bag or reusable tea bag, place in your bottle of tequila and allow to infuse overnight. Taste it and continue to infuse until it tastes as you would like, then discard the saffron.

Menus

The Spanish Pantry is more than a collection of recipes; it's about the memories we create when we share a meal. Whether it's a casual lunch with family, a long, lazy brunch with friends, or a lively evening of tapas, the table is where some of life's best moments happen. These menus are here to help you turn simple, delicious ingredients into meals that bring people together and linger in their minds long after the plates are cleared.

The magic of these 12 pantry staples is their versatility. They're the building blocks for so many Spanish flavours and can shape meals for every occasion. That's why I've put together a collection of menus to make life easier and more inspiring: a tapas menu for sharing and nibbling, a hearty lunch, an inviting dinner, a relaxed brunch, a summery spread and a vibrant vegetarian feast.

Each menu is designed to flow naturally from one dish to the next, with plenty of variety in flavours and textures. And because we all want to enjoy the company as much as the food, I've added a few tips for planning and prepping ahead, so you can focus on the people around you rather than rushing in the kitchen.

For me, the most special part of cooking is what happens when the food is served – plates passed around, glasses raised, stories shared. I hope these menus inspire you to create your own moments like this, whether it's a spontaneous gathering or a carefully planned celebration.

So, dive into your Spanish pantry, pick a menu, and cook up something unforgettable. After all, the best memories are made around the table.

Lunch menu

(serves 6)

Aubergine and bean dip (page 198)

Roast pumpkin and chickpeas with lemon and oregano (page 181)

Sobrasada rice with crispy artichokes (page 152)

Simple orange ice cream (page 134)

Up to a week before

Make the Simple orange ice cream and keep in the freezer

The day before

Make the Aubergine and bean dip, store in the fridge and allow to come to room temperature before serving

On the day

Cook the roast pumpkin and chickpeas with lemon and oregano

Cook the Sobrasada rice with crispy artichokes

Finish the Aubergine and bean dip

Dinner menu

(serves 8)

Spanish daisy cocktail (recipe × 8) (page 237)

Buñuelos de Manchego (page 101)

Saffron salt with seared scallops (recipe × 2) (page 232)

Rare sliced rib of beef with almond and tarragon salsa (page 116)

Roast potatoes with Manchego and pepper crust (recipe × 2) (page 96)

Warm olive oil and almond cake with preserved peaches (page 108)

Two days before

Make the saffron infused gin (if not buying)

Make the peaches for the Warm olive oil and almond cake

On the day

Make the Buñuelos de Manchego

Make the Saffron salt with seared scallops

Make the Rare sliced rib of beef with almond and tarragon salsa

Make the Roast potatoes with Manchego and pepper crust

Finish the Warm olive oil and almond cake

Finish the Spanish daisy cocktail

Tapas menu

(serves 6)

Citrus and lemon thyme Spanish gin and tonic
(recipe × 2) (page 149)

Griddled spring onion tortilla (page 19)

Pan con tomate verde (recipe × 2) (page 41)

Tomato-cured seabass and cockles (page 49)

Croquetas de chorizo (page 74)

Gilda's devilled eggs (page 62)

Mini chocolate-coated almond ice creams
(page 119)

Two days before

Make the Mini chocolate-coated almond ice creams
and store in the freezer

Make the syrup for the Citrus and lemon thyme
Spanish gin and tonic and store in the fridge

The day before

Make the base for the Croquetas de chorizo and
store in the fridge

Boil the eggs for the Gilda's devilled eggs

On the day

Make the Griddled spring onion tortilla

Make the Pan con tomate verde

Make the Tomato-cured seabass and cockles

Finish the Croquetas de chorizo

Finish the Gilda's devilled eggs

Finish the Citrus and lemon thyme Spanish
gin and tonic

Brunch menu

(serves 4)

Tortilla vaga (page 72)

Poached eggs with chorizo and broad beans
(page 83)

Warm gigante beans on toast (page 195)

Saffron and honey torrijas (page 229)

The day before

Cook the beans for the Warm gigante beans on
toast and store in the fridge

Infuse the milk for the Saffron and honey torrijas and
store in the fridge

On the day

Make the Tortilla vaga

Make the Poached eggs with chorizo and broad
beans

Reheat the beans for the Warm gigante beans on
toast

Finish the Saffron and honey torrijas

Vegetarian menu

(serves 4–6)

Ajo blanco with roasted grapes (page 113)

Pisto-stuffed tomatoes (page 46)

Confit lemon with courgette and requesón (page 140)

Garlic and Manchego coca (page 95)

Salted arroz con leche (page 160)

The day before

Make the soup element of the Ajo blanco with roasted grapes

Prepare the confit lemon of the Confit lemon with courgette and requesón

Cook the Salted arroz con leche (do not add the cream yet) and store in the fridge

On the day

Make the Pisto-stuffed tomatoes

Make the Garlic and Manchego coca

Finish the Confit lemon with courgette and requesón

Finish the Ajo blanco with roasted grapes

Finish the Salted arroz con leche

Summer lunch party

(serves 8–10)

Salted anchovy and onion tart (page 26)

Jamón serrano and watermelon salad with honey and basil (recipe × 2) (page 207)

Saffron and prawn croquetas (page 226)

Chickpea flatbreads with mussels (recipe × 2) (page 175)

Wild rice salad with home-smoked mackerel (recipe × 2) (page 162)

Caramelised almonds with dulce de leche semifreddo (page 114)

Two days before

Make the semifreddo of the Caramelised almonds with dulce de leche semifreddo and store in the freezer

The day before

Make the rice for the Wild rice salad with home-smoked mackerel and store in the fridge

Make the base for the Saffron and prawn croquetas

On the day

Make the Salted anchovy and onion tart

Make the Chickpea flatbreads with mussels

Make the Jamón serrano and watermelon salad with honey and basil

Finish the Saffron and prawn croquetas

Index

Acknowledgements

This book is for my mum, Isabel. Her patience, incredible cooking, and the way she always kept our pantry stocked with the best local ingredients have been an inspiration.

A big thank you to my partner Peter for his steadfast support, thoughtful editing and constant encouragement. You keep me focused every step of the way.

To my family – your love and support mean everything to me.

I'm so grateful to Kate Pollard and the team at Quadrille for believing in me and enjoying my passion for Spanish cuisine. A special thanks to food stylist Lizzie Kamenetzky and photographer Emma Lee for bringing my recipes to life so beautifully in this book. Thank you also to Clare Skeats for the design, and Becky Baur for the stunning lemon painting on the cover.

And to my amazing team across all my businesses – your hard work and dedication make it all possible. Thank you for striving for excellence every day.

Thank you also to Amandine Dagand and Juan Gacia Pizarro for your help with bringing things together.

Last, but by all means not least, to all my customers and the various companies I work with – your trust and collaboration inspire me to keep creating and growing. Thank you for being a part of this journey.

About the author

José Pizarro, widely known as 'The Godfather of Spanish Cooking in the UK', hails from the picturesque rural village of Talaván in Cáceres, Extremadura. José trained in some of Spain's finest kitchens, ultimately becoming Head Chef at the Michelin-starred El Mesón de Doña Filo, before moving to London over 26 years ago. In the UK, he worked at various prestigious Spanish establishments including Gaudi, Eyre Brothers, and was co-founder of Brindisa restaurants, where he became the Executive Chef.

In 2011, José opened his first solo venture, José Tapas Bar on Bermondsey Street, inspired by the bustling tapas bars of Barcelona it is celebrated for its daily market-driven menu and exceptional range of sherries. That same year, he launched Pizarro, a restaurant named after his grandfather, which has earned numerous accolades such as the World Food Awards Restaurant of the Year, and *Food and Travel* Magazine's Best Restaurant in London. José has since expanded his culinary business to the City of London with José Pizarro Bar Plaza; to central London with José Pizarro at the Royal Academy of Arts; to Surrey with The Swan Inn in Esher, and his first international restaurant, José by Pizarro at the Conrad Hilton in Abu Dhabi. Most recently, he opened Lolo, a stylish all-day dining destination on Bermondsey Street, and Iris, an exclusive seaside property in Andalusia offering luxury food-and-travel experiences.

José's philosophy centres on fresh, seasonal produce and mastering simplicity, creating dishes that celebrate traditional Spanish flavours while elevating the ingredients to new heights. His charm and passion for food made him a beloved figure on TV shows such as BBC One's *Saturday Kitchen*, ITV's *This Morning*, Channel 4's *Sunday Brunch* and *James Martin's Saturday Morning*.

An accomplished author, José's critically acclaimed cookbooks include *Seasonal Spanish Food* (2009), *Spanish Flavours* (2012), *Basque* (2016), *Catalonia* (2017), *Andalusia* (2019, compact edition in 2023) and *The Spanish Home Kitchen* (2022). His latest book reflects the same ethos that defines his career: the joy of bringing people together through simple, flavourful food.

José has earned numerous prestigious awards, including the *Gran Maestro De La Orden De Isabel La Católica* from King Felipe VI of Spain, the *Elle* Gourmet Award 2024 for International Chef, and the *La Medalla de Extremadura*, the highest honour in the region. He was also named Chef of the Year by *Food and Travel Magazine* in 2022 and by *FT Magazine* in 2019. Whether through his restaurants, books or TV appearances, José continues to inspire with an unwavering passion for sharing the heart and soul of Spanish cuisine.

Quadrille, Penguin Random House UK,
One Embassy Gardens, 8 Viaduct Gardens,
London SW11 7BW

Quadrille Publishing Limited is part of the Penguin Random House
group of companies whose addresses can be found at
global.penguinrandomhouse.com

Published by Quadrille in 2025

www.penguin.co.uk

A CIP catalogue record for this book is available from the British Library

ISBN 9781784889753

10 9 8 7 6 5 4 3 2 1

Publishing Director: Kate Pollard
Photographer and Prop Stylist: Emma Lee
Cover Artwork: Becky Baur
Designer: Clare Skeats
Food Stylist: Lizzie Kamenetzky
Copy Editor: Wendy Hobson
Proofreader: Kathy Steer
Production Controller: Sabeena Atchia
Colour reproduction by p2d
Printed in China by C&C Offset Printing Co., Ltd.

The authorised representative in the EEA is Penguin Random House Ireland,
Morrison Chambers, 32 Nassau Street, Dublin D02 YH68.